REAL JUSTICE:

FOURTEEN AND SENTENCED TO DEATH

• • •

THE STORY OF STEVEN TRUSCOTT

BILL SWAN

LORIMER

JAMES LORIMER & COMPANY LTD., PUBLISHERS
TORONTO

James Lorimer & Company Ltd., Publishers, acknowledges the support of the Ontario Arts Council. We acknowledge the financial support of the Government of Canada through the Canada Book Fund for our publishing activities. We acknowledge the support of the Canada Council for the Arts which last year invested $24.3 million in writing and publishing throughout Canada. We acknowledge the Government of Ontario through the Ontario Media Development Corporation's Ontario Book Initiative.

ONTARIO ARTS COUNCIL
CONSEIL DES ARTS DE L'ONTARIO

Canada Council
for the Arts

Library and Archives Canada Cataloguing in Publication

Swan, Bill, 1939-
    Real justice : fourteen and sentenced to death : the story of Steven Truscott / Bill Swan.

Real justice)
Includes bibliographical references and index.
Issued also in electronic format.
ISBN 978-1-4594-0075-7 (bound).--ISBN 978-1-4594-0074-0 (pbk.)

    1. Truscott, Steven, 1945-. 2. Harper, Lynne, 1946-1959.
3. Murder--Ontario--Clinton--Juvenile literature. 4. Judicial error--Ontario--Clinton--Juvenile literature. I. Title.

HV6535.C33C55 2012   j364.152'30971322   C2011-908689-1

James Lorimer & Company Ltd.,
Publishers
317 Adelaide Street West, Suite 1002
Toronto, ON, Canada
M5V 1P9
www.lorimer.ca

Distributed in the United States by:
Orca Book Publishers
P.O. Box 468
Custer, WA USA
98240-0468

Printed and bound in Canada.
Manufactured by Friesens Corporation in Altona, Manitoba, Canada in February 2012
Job #72998

*TO "TEED" MACKINNON, WHO CONVINCED ME YEARS AGO
THAT STEVEN WAS INNOCENT; TO ALL THOSE "IN THE
SYSTEM" WHO GOT TO KNOW STEVEN AND SOFTEN HIS
LOAD; AND TO STEVEN TRUSCOTT. THE REST OF US
SIMPLY CANNOT IMAGINE.*

CONTENTS

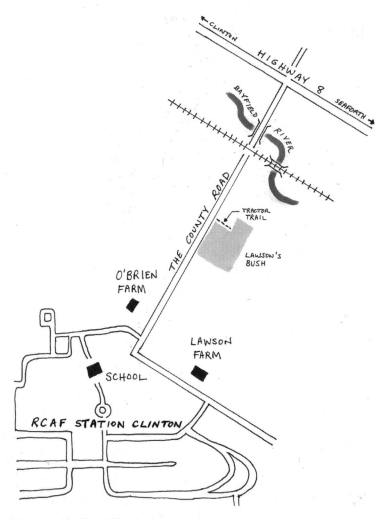

Map created by Daniel Mansfield

NOTE: Although most dialogue is quoted directly from testimony at trials or statements given to police, some has been recreated based on transcripts, interviews, or other documentation to improve context and narrative flow.

INTRODUCTION BY DOUGLAS OATES

When I was in the fifth grade, a boy in grade seven at my school was convicted of rape and murder and sentenced to be hanged. His name was Steven Truscott.

I can't imagine what Steven went through in the forty-seven years until his name was cleared.

I was eleven going on twelve years old that summer. On the night in question, I saw Steven and Lynne Harper together at a time and at a place that should have proved Steven was innocent.

I did what my mother and father had taught me to do: I told the truth. I told it over and over — to police, to a preliminary hearing, and at the trial. In spite of that, the judge and jury decided that I and all the defence witnesses who did not bend to the Crown's theory were involved in a conspiracy and that each witness was a liar.

My brother, Alan, and another boy, Gordon Logan, also testified on Steven's behalf. They were branded liars, too. Karen Daum, then nine years old, also told police she had seen Steven and Lynne. She wasn't even called on to testify.

Several times, police asked me to change my story. I stuck to what I knew to be the truth. Imagine, then, that in spite of telling the truth, you learn that a guy you know to be innocent has been found guilty — and sentenced to hang.

Repeat that: *to hang.*

Nothing can prepare you for that shock. Now, fifty-three years later, I can tell you that it took me a long time to deal with it. For years, I had issues in dealing with authority. My trust in the justice system was shaken. No, worse than shaken: broken.

However, others paid attention and persevered. Finally, someone did listen and justice was served. If I had to do it again, I would tell the truth and keep doing so until someone paid attention. Justice is too important to be broken.

DOUGLAS OATES
EDMONTON, AB

THE SENTENCE

GODERICH, ON
SEPTEMBER 30, 1959 - 10:55 P.M.

The judge waited until the jury settled into their seats. The wooden floors and chairs creaked.

"Do you find the prisoner at the bar guilty or not guilty?" asked a court official.

The jury foreman, rising, said, "We find the defendant guilty as charged, with a plea for mercy."

"The prisoner stand up," said the judge.

Slowly, a boy rose to his feet. Instead of being in court, he should have been starting the eighth grade. He was fourteen years old.

The judge looked down at him.

"Steven Murray Truscott, have you anything to say? Why the sentence of this court should not be passed upon you according to law?"

"No," Steven replied.

"Steven Murray Truscott, I have no alternative but to pass the following sentence upon you.

"The jury has found you guilty after a fair trial.

"The sentence of this court upon you is that you be taken from here to the place from whence you came.

"And there be kept in close confinement until Tuesday, the eighth day of December, 1959.

"And upon that day and date you be taken to the place of execution.

"And that you there be hanged by the neck until you are dead.

"And may the Lord have mercy upon your soul."

1

CHAPTER ONE

LYNNE HARPER IS MISSING

WEDNESDAY, JUNE 10, 1959 - 7:55 A.M.

When fourteen-year-old Steven Truscott came down for breakfast that morning, sleepy-eyed, he could not have imagined that three days later he would face a murder charge.

He grabbed a piece of toast his mother had prepared. His fifteen-year-old brother, Ken, had been up first. Steve hoped Ken had left some cornflakes.

Steve was in grade seven and was the best athlete in his school at the Royal Canadian Air Force base in Clinton, Ontario, where his father was a warrant officer.

A sharp knock sounded on the side door. Steve's mother, Doris, walked the two steps down from the kitchen to the landing and answered the door. She did not recognize the man who stood outside.

"I was wondering if your boys had seen Lynne?" the man asked. He looked worried and shifted nervously.

"Lynne who?" asked Mrs. Truscott.

"Lynne Harper."

She recognized him now: Lynne's father. Mrs. Truscott had met Mr. Harper once before, several months ago, but did not make the connection right away. On the air base, families and people moved in and out often. However, the name was familiar. Lynne was Steven's classmate.

Mrs. Truscott called to her oldest son, Ken, who was on the basement stairs, shining his shoes. "Did you see Lynne Harper last night?"

Ken didn't even bother to look up. He was in high school and seventh graders meant nothing to him.

"No," he replied.

In the kitchen, Steve could hear the exchange. Now his mother turned to him.

"Steve?" asked his mother.

"Yes, I gave her a lift to number eight highway," Steve replied, rummaging for a cereal bowl.

Mrs. Truscott beckoned to Steve to step closer to Mr. Harper. "Come down here." Steve stepped down from the kitchen and faced Mr. Harper with only a screen door between them.

Mr. Harper asked again if Steve had seen Lynne.

"I gave her a lift to number eight highway," Steve repeated.

"Where did you give her a lift?" Mr. Harper asked again.

"From the school down to the number eight highway," Steve replied. This was the third time Mr. Harper had asked the question. To Steve, it appeared that he did not want to accept the answer. The highway was about 1.6 km north of the school on the county road. It was past the railway tracks and over the bridge across the Bayfield River.

After an awkward silence, Steve added that he then returned to the bridge, where others were playing in the river. From the bridge, he said, he saw Lynne hitchhiking and then get into a grey car.

Mr. Harper took a deep breath. "Oh, my God!" he said. He turned and slumped away.

He had reason to be frightened. Lynne, twelve years old, had not returned home the night before.

Police had been called and the search for a missing person had begun.

• • •

Everyone at school that morning knew that Lynne Harper was missing.

Air Vice Marshall Hugh Campbell School was a

twelve-room school on the air base. One-room rural schools were common in 1959. In size, this school matched schools in the suburbs of Toronto.

Still, the school was small enough to buzz with the news.

In Mr. Edgar's classroom, the empty seat near the teacher's desk drew everyone's attention. Earlier in the school year, Lynne had been moved to a seat near the front of the classroom. She was friendly, but talked a lot.

Steve sat near the back right-hand corner of the room. A couple of desks away sat his buddy, Arnold "Butch" George. Across the room sat thirteen-year-old Jocelyne Gaudet, a girl with her hair in ringlets.

By morning recess, the police had arrived. One by one, students were called to the staff room. Police wanted to talk to anyone who had seen Lynne the previous evening.

When it was his turn, Steve told his story to police: he had met Lynne at the school, and near 7:30 p.m. he had given her a ride to the highway.

She had been angry with her parents, she told him. They had ridden along the county road, over the bridge near the swimming hole. He had crossed the bridge. He had left her at Highway 8. She had been heading to visit ponies at the white house on the highway, a few hundred feet east of where Steve had left her.

Steven said he then returned to the bridge and looked back toward the highway. He had seen a car stop, likely a 1959 Chev, he said, with a yellow licence plate or sticker. The car pulled onto the county road from the highway, then pulled back at an angle, still pointing east.

From the bridge, 400 metres away, he saw Lynne get into the front seat.

Police were obviously very interested in Steve's account of the previous evening. That was no mystery. He had seen her last.

Steve did his best to provide details of the ride from the school to the highway. He was helpful. Friendly.

Those who knew Steve would have expected that. He was the top athlete in his school; even the younger kids admired him. He was 1.75 metres in height, and towered over most of his classmates. Light brown hair, hazel eyes, an infectious smile . . . it was no wonder girls liked him.

He was not an A student, but he was no failure, either. He achieved Bs and Cs — enough to get by. He liked to be active: fishing, swimming, riding his unique three-speed bike everywhere. When the school football team won the Little Grey Cup the previous fall, Steve was identified by the local newspaper as the star of the team.

At Bob Lawson's farm across the road, he often helped with chores. "Others would fool around," Bob Lawson said. "But if I were in my welding shop, Steve paid attention. He liked to learn how to do things."

At home in his basement that year, Steve had built a go-cart. Instead of the usual axel pivot for steering, he had figured out a way to articulate the steering so each front wheel swivelled together, but independently. Like a real car.

In their hunt for Lynne, police tried to track down anyone who had been on the county road that evening.

The county road to the bridge near the highway was a popular place. A number of people, kids and adults, had walked, biked, and rode along that stretch that night. The heat and humidity — it was an unseasonal 31 degrees Celsius — had sent many to the river to fish, swim, or just find relief.

Lynne's parents originally thought she may have hitchhiked. In 1959, hitchhiking was not unusual. It wasn't a smart thing to do, and parents discouraged it. But Lynne and many of her friends had hitchhiked before. To town. Across the base. To the highway.

Lynne had argued with her parents about going swimming in the pool on the base. She had a grandmother in

Port Stanley. Her parents told police that perhaps she had fled there in anger.

Many twelve- to fourteen-year-olds go missing. Surely Lynne would be like most and show up tired and hungry a day or two later.

Wouldn't she?

2

CHAPTER TWO

STEVE HELPS OUT

WEDNESDAY, JUNE 10 - 5:30 P.M.

A police car was waiting in front of his home when Steve returned next afternoon from the Holmesville quarry. The school had been given a half-holiday to attend the Clinton Fair. Instead of going to the fair, however, Steve had gone swimming in the deep, cool quarry waters with several buddies.

If Steve felt nervous about the police interest in his story, he gave no outward signs. Could he help them some more? the officers asked.

His mother went with him, riding in the rear seat of the police car. Steve sat in the front with the officer, Constable Donald Trumbley. They drove past the school, then headed north on the county road, past Lawson's woods, over the railroad track to the bridge.

At the north end of the bridge over the Bayfield

River, Constable Trumbley parked the cruiser.

He and Corporal Liscombe from the Goderich OPP detachment asked Steve where he had been when he saw Lynne get into a car. Steve showed them.

The officers noted that from that point, about 400 metres from the highway, it was impossible to see the licence plate numbers on cars moving on the highway.

Steve repeated that he had not said he could see a licence plate number. He had seen only what appeared to be a yellow licence plate on a car parked at the intersection.

His mother suggested that perhaps he had seen a coloured bumper sticker. The Truscott family car had such a sticker from Storybook Gardens in London.

Steve and his mother were taken home shortly after.

After supper, Steve returned to the bridge. This time he was with his close friend, Arnold "Butch" George. The two joined three other friends seeking refuge from the heat.

Idle banter and talk of the missing girl turned to teasing.

"I heard you had Lynne in the woods," Paul Desjardine said to Steve.

"Who told you that?" Steven snapped.

Steven had reason to bristle. Butch had made up a

story the night before about Steve hunting for calves in the woods with Lynne. The story began as teasing. Butch admitted he had never seen Steve with Lynne the night before. Yet he willingly repeated the yarn.

Several times that day, people had mentioned the made-up story. With a serious police investigation underway, Steve did not find the tale funny.

"Butch said you were," said Paul.

Butch was ten feet below them under the bridge, throwing rocks.

"I didn't take her into the woods," Steve replied. "I didn't." Still on his bike, he leaned over the bridge railing and raised his voice so Butch could hear.

"I didn't take Lynne into the woods, did I, Butch?"

His voice echoed off the concrete, the rocks, and the water.

"No, you had her at the side of the bush looking for a cow and calf." Butch replied, his voice echoing from under the bridge.

The joke may have originated from a happening two weeks before, when Steve and his buddy Leslie Spilsbury had found a cow and its calf in Lawson's woods. That had made the two boys into school heroes. And that, for the time and place, made Steve a chick magnet.

Hearing that Steve had given Lynne a ride on his

bike, Butch may have woven the stories together. The previous evening, Butch had entertained some friends with the story. The guys had jeered — they did not believe him. He kept repeating the story as though it meant something. But in a final statement to police, Butch admitted that he had made up the tale shortly after leaving the swimming hole — without having seen either Lynne or Steve.

The talk on the bridge that night, twenty-four hours after Lynne had vanished, drifted to more important things: turtles, rocks, swimming, and the heat.

No one could have predicted what would happen when Lynne was found, and how police would twist Butch's teasing into a horror story.

3

CHAPTER THREE

THE SEARCH FOR LYNNE

THURSDAY, JUNE 11 - 1:30 P.M.

Steve and his classmates in Maitland Edgar's mixed grade seven and eight class could see the search party on the road in front of Lawson's farm.

The sight of the 125 men told everyone that this was now a serious matter.

Lynne had been missing for forty-one hours.

Two seats up from Steve, Butch craned his neck. Across the room, Jocelyne Gaudet stretched to get a better look at the searchers.

None could avoid seeing Lynne's empty desk.

Many young teens go missing each year. Most return home or show up at the homes of friends or relatives.

A small number are never seen again, disappearing as though abducted by aliens.

A few are found, weeks or months later in some

deserted area, a pile of bones in a shallow grave.

If it is believed that a missing person has been driven away in a car, then a search where the person was last seen is not worth the effort. An automobile could whisk a victim hundreds of kilometres away in a couple of hours. This search meant that police thought Lynne had not been taken away in a car. This meant they already had some doubts about Steve's story.

It also meant that police believed she was dead.

The searchers did not dwell on that possibility, and what that would mean.

Many grown men were about to find out.

Across the road, farmer Bob Lawson stood on the lawn by his house and watched as the searchers began. It was a sad story, this missing girl. But he could not help but be amused by the search party.

They stepped across his fences, stretching the fence wire. Didn't these city slickers know that crossing a fence should be done at the posts? Apparently not. It was unclear to him who was in charge of the search. One thing he did know: no one had asked his permission, even though it was his fences they trampled.

The fields were filled with men. That morning, Corporal Sayeau of the OPP, with the help of the air base commander, had organized a search party of 250 men into two groups. One group was to cover the land west of the county road, through O'Brien's farm. The other group was to cover the land east of the county road, through Lawson's farm to the highway.

The eastern group started after lunch, before the western group had gathered. They advanced north on Lawson's land, spread about three metres apart.

They trampled over crops barely poking through the ground. Not all the searchers knew enough to step lightly between the rows.

In the pasture, they stepped around cow pies.

Eventually, the searchers made their way toward the woods at the back of the Lawson farm.

By then, the school children had turned their attention back to their books. Flies buzzed at the classroom windows, struggling to get out.

Some students fanned themselves with workbooks. The heat, in a room with thirty students and no air conditioning, pressed on them.

• • •

Step by step, looking left and right from time to time, the men in the line moved like a parade square formation advancing in review order.

While in the open fields, the searchers found it easy to keep together. In Lawson's woods, the line lost its precision. Up and down the line, men stepped over the fence into the woods.

Footing in the woods was uneven. Logs, piles of brush, and fallen trees barred the way. The searchers drifted, the distance between them now as much as six metres. Keeping track of other searchers was harder. Even in the shade, the heat of the humid air clung to them.

Grumbles and curses sounded up and down the line. Decayed branches snapped underfoot. Searchers pushed away brush, branches, anything under which someone might hide.

Or hide something.

Lieutenant Joseph Leger and Corporal George Edens were among the search party. In the woods, they swatted mosquitoes. Step by step, they kept their place in the line of searchers. They stepped around a tree and checked their place in formation.

Leger was the first to see her; Edens came around the tree almost at the same time.

Leger alerted the other searcher. "There she is," he called out.

4

CHAPTER FOUR

LYNNE IS FOUND

THURSDAY, JUNE 11 - 1:30 P.M.

Lynne Harper lay on her back in a hollow at the base of a clump of trees in the woods. Three tree branches lay crosswise over her body. They were about the size of a man's thumb and had been twisted from nearby trees.

She was naked except for her blood-soaked undershirt. Her blouse had been ripped and partly removed. Her left arm had been removed from its sleeve, and the blouse was tied tightly around her neck.

Her left leg was straight. Her right leg was bent slightly.

Her left arm rested across her stomach. Her right arm was bent at the elbow and her right hand rested beside her head.

To the right of her head, a red headband, two shoes,

socks, and shorts lay neatly. One shoe lay on its side. The socks, ankle-length, had each been rolled neatly, as though partially pulled down and partly rolled. Mud splattered her shorts. The zipper had been carefully closed and neatly folded. Her panties were found several metres to the northeast as though dropped carelessly.

A few centimetres from each of her feet, dirt had been pushed up in small mounds. One searcher claimed to make out a smudged footprint made by a shoe with crepe soles.

Not far away, a fourth branch had been twisted but not completely severed. The twisted portion was nearly seven feet above the ground.

Flies buzzed around her body. Maggots had begun to appear.

She had been strangled with her own blouse and raped. That's what they called it then: rape.

Today, Canadian law refers to it as sexual assault.

Searchers gathered round. Some gagged.

Many searchers had children of their own who were the same age as Lynne. For most, it was their first sight of a dead body.

Flying Officer Sage hurried to the spot. He was the officer in charge of this part of the search group.

A senior officer soon arrived. Over the objections of

Flying Officer Sage, he ordered searchers to cover the body. Jackets and shirts were thrown on the branches, supposedly to hide the half-naked body from curious eyes.

Forensic science in the 1950s was not as advanced as today. Still, examination by microscope had been known to match fibres. Criminals had been convicted on such evidence. Covering the body was a mistake.

More than a hundred searchers milled about, some within two feet of the body. Searchers were ordered to leave, and directed to a tractor trail a couple dozen steps further north, along the far edge of the woods. From there, it was a short distance to the county road, less than the length of a football field.

Where the tractor trail met the county road, Corporal Edens noted spin marks from car tires — a pair of grooves a metre long. To him, it appeared that a car had lurched up the incline from the trail to the road, spinning its rear tires onto the pavement.

Shortly after they reached the county road, Lieutenant Leger and Corporal Edens were ordered to return to the woods. By then, one of farmer Lawson's neighbours had been sent on his motorcycle to fetch police.

Corporal Sayeau of the Goderich detachment of the OPP arrived at 2:08 p.m. and took charge. If anyone thought it curious that the police were not visible during the search, he did not speak up.

The search for Lynne Harper had become a murder investigation.

CHAPTER FIVE

THE PATHOLOGIST AT WORK

THURSDAY, JUNE 11 - 4:45 P.M.

The first role of the police at the scene was to gather evidence. This task fell to Corporal John Erskine, the district identification officer for the OPP.

Erskine arrived on the scene at about 4 p.m. Lugging his heavy, large-format camera, Erskine recorded the scene, taking photos from several angles.

About fifteen minutes before 5 p.m., Dr. John L. Penistan of Stratford arrived. A pipe-smoking man in his mid-forties, he served as the district pathologist. His official duty was to perform an autopsy to determine the cause of death.

In all matters medical, he would be expected to testify in court. His findings would be treated as official expert opinion.

Between them, the police and Dr. Penistan began a

more accurate measurement of the body and the setting. Her undershirt under her left shoulder was soaked in blood. Her blouse, on the other hand, had none. The body bore other marks of violence. Dr. Penistan ordered the body to be lifted so blood samples could be taken from the ground. Following a preliminary examination at the scene, the body was removed for autopsy at a funeral home in Clinton.

The autopsy could have — some argue *should* have — been performed in a specially prepared and equipped room. With proper lighting and equipment, the autopsy might have provided more facts. But transporting a body costs money. The budget did not cover that cost.

The autopsy room at the funeral home was about the size of a small bedroom. In this room, three men surrounded a metal table lit by one overhead light. An extra lamp was brought in to provide better lighting.

Dr. Penistan sealed the stomach contents in a jar to examine later. A cursory glance revealed vegetables, perhaps some meat, all in the beginning stages of digestion. At the time, Dr. Penistan noted that based on the stomach contents, Lynne had probably died about one or two hours after the meal had been eaten.

Lynne had a long scratch on her left leg, reaching from a few inches above the kneecap down the front of the lower leg to the top of the foot. Dried blood indicated the wound had bled. Dr. Penistan thought it had occurred just before death.

The knot in the blouse under Lynne's jaw was too tight to untie. To remove it, Dr. Penistan cut through it with scissors. He handed the two pieces of the blouse to Sgt. Erskine to be used as a future court exhibit.

Later, it was discovered that a large portion of the blouse, a piece about 25 cm by 20 cm, was missing. No one knows if this portion was dropped on the floor of the autopsy room or it if had been missing before the autopsy, perhaps taken as a souvenir by the killer.

On such shaky grounds, the search began for the answer to a question that remains unanswered to this day:

Who killed Lynne Harper?

6

CHAPTER SIX

STEVE HELPS THE POLICE

FRIDAY, JUNE 12 - 1:30 P.M.

The next day, everyone knew that Lynne's body had been found. As they did every Friday morning, Steven and the rest of Mr. Edgar's class discussed "current events." Could anything be more current than the murder of a classmate?

In a classroom in which Lynne's empty desk was now the focal point, Mr. Edgar explained what is meant by murder.

One student asked about the different degrees of murder. Mr. Edgar explained that the most serious was *first-degree murder* — usually one that had been planned ahead of time. A death occurring during a sexual assault, even if unplanned, is also first-degree murder. It is unlikely the teacher mentioned that fact. Anyone convicted of first-degree murder, at that time, faced the death penalty.

Steve took part in the discussion.

Shortly after morning recess, the principal called Steve to the office. He was to meet Inspector Graham of the OPP.

Steve had already talked to the police five times in three days. What more could they want? he wondered. With his father, Steve met Inspector Graham at the base guardhouse. A girl had been murdered, and Steve felt it was his duty to provide what help he could. His father had been named 1959 Man of the Year on the base for his work with young people. To both father and son, helping was second nature.

Inspector Harold Graham, a big, tough, no-nonsense police officer, wore his authority like an overdose of aftershave.

He had spent the evening — and a good portion of the night — reviewing interview notes from the officers. Already he knew the stories of everyone the officers had talked to as part of their investigation.

But those statements had been made to help find a missing person. He was now in charge of a murder investigation.

"Since Steven was the last person known to have seen Lynne Harper alive, it is important and desirable that we get a detailed account of what he knew about her," Graham told Steve and his father.

A stenographer from the air base was brought in to take notes. In other police interviews, the officers had taken their own handwritten notes.

"For the record, tell us your name and age," said Inspector Graham.

"My name is Steve Truscott. I am fourteen years old," Steve replied.

"What school do you attend?"

"AVM Hugh Campbell School."

"Where do you live?"

"Two Quebec Road."

"How long have you known Lynne Harper?"

"One or two years."

"Tell us what happened that night."

Steve replied, "I met her up at the corner of the road going round the school on my bicycle."

"Where were you going?"

"I was going towards the river to see some of the boys who were going fishing."

"And then what?"

"She asked if she could have a ride down to the highway."

Inspector Graham paused. He had read this in the previous statements.

"And she got on the handlebars?"

"She got on the crossbar," Steve replied, "and I gave her a ride."

Inspector Graham sighed.

"And what did you talk about on your little trip?" he asked.

"She asked where we went fishing. I said down at the river, and there is also a trout stream at number eight highway."

"Is that all?"

"She asked me if I knew people in the little white house."

"Did you give her a ride to this white house? The one on Highway 8?"

"I took her to the highway and let her off."

"Surely you talked about more than fishing and the white house."

"She said she was mad at her mother 'cause she didn't let her go swimming. That is all she said on the way down."

"And how did she seem to you?"

"She wasn't mad. She was carefree."

Steve had repeated this story many times in the past few days. When he had returned to the school that evening after dropping Lynne off, his friends had teased him about feeding Lynne "to the fishes." That was no longer funny.

"Tell us again about this car," said Inspector Graham. 'The one that supposedly picked her up."

"I got up on the bridge and looked around to see if she got a ride, and a grey Chev picked her up."

"Was she hitchhiking?"

"She had her thumb out. A car swerved in off the edge of the road and pulled out. That's why I noticed it had odd licence plates."

"What was odd about the plate?" asked the inspector.

"It was a yellow background."

"Which way was the car going?"

"Toward Seaforth."

"That would be east?"

Steve nodded.

"Describe this car again."

This time it was Steve who sighed. How many times had he told this?

"It was a grey '59 Chev, solid grey, quite a bit of chrome, white-wall tires. She got in the front seat and the car pulled away going toward Seaforth."

The questioning had spun in circles going over and over the same story.

Suddenly, the inspector changed.

"Are you interested in girls?" he asked.

Steve blinked. "Some."

"Were you ever out with her?"

"No."

"Why not?"

"There was no one interested in her. There was none of them liked her too much. She was sort of bossy in school."

Inspector Graham fell silent for a moment. He shuffled through his papers and pages of handwritten notes.

"That'll be all for now," he said. "Miss Jervis will type up your statement and you'll be asked later to come in and sign it."

• • •

Inspector Graham talked to three other children that afternoon.

Eleven-year-old Dougie Oates told Inspector Graham what he had told the other officer the day after Lynne disappeared: He had been hunting turtles on the bridge and saw Steve and Lynne on Steve's bicycle heading toward the highway.

"Are you sure?"

Dougie was sure.

Inspector Graham also had Butch George brought in.

Had he seen Steve and Lynne that night? asked the inspector.

"I went to the swimming hole at about 7 p.m.," Butch said. "I was there about fifteen minutes when Steve and Lynne biked north."

A third student, Jocelyne Gaudet, thirteen, had a much more riveting story to tell.

She said Steve had invited her to look for calves in the woods — the same night that Lynne disappeared.

"Are you sure?"

Jocelyne told the officer that she had been looking for Lynne that evening near the woods where Lynne's body was found. Interested, Inspector Graham called in Constable Trumbley to take down a more detailed statement from Jocelyne.

Now with a receptive audience, Jocelyne expanded her story. Steve not only invited her to look for calves that evening, she told the officer, but had asked her to meet him where the county road met the tractor trail.

She said she had waited on the county road, and then walked in on the tractor trail. This was only a few metres from where Lynne's body was found. This, she said, gave her a feeling of unease.

Shortly after, Inspector Graham ordered that Steve Truscott be brought in again for questioning.

"Preferably without his parents," he said. He wanted some time alone with the boy.

Steve Truscott was now the first and only name on the list of murder suspects.

7

CHAPTER SEVEN

STEVE IS ARRESTED

FRIDAY, JUNE 12 - 6:50 P.M.

The heat hung heavy over Bob Lawson's farm. Temperatures all week had been sizzling. But Bob could smell a change in the air. Cooler air was on the way.

But cooler air meant thunderstorms. That could mean crop damage.

Bob Lawson was a twenty-two-year-old farmer. He lived directly across the road from the air force base on a 150-acre mixed farm, where he still lives today. He raised a few chickens and some pigs, and harvested firewood and hardwood from the woods on the back fifty acres of his land. He had forty head of cattle.

Lawson's farm was a kid magnet. And Farmer Lawson welcomed them. In an innocent time filled mostly with innocent, decent people, Bob Lawson was the cream of the crop.

Friday after supper, Steve headed for Bob's farm. He felt troubled after his interview with Inspector Graham that morning.

At the farm, Steve rode with Lawson on the tractor to the nearby field. With rain threatening, Bob wanted to harvest as much as possible before the promised storm.

The talkative Lawson and Steve were both quiet that evening. The events of the week had been stunning. Steve found comfort in the isolation of the farm and the company of this young farmer.

While Lawson harvested the field, Steve rested on a nearby rock. Later, when Lawson looked up, Steve was gone.

At 6:50 p.m., Steve was walking down the farm lane. A black and white police car drove up. Many rural residents referred to a police cruiser as a Holstein, after the black and white breed of dairy cattle common in the area. Others referred to it as a skunk car. Same colours, different image.

Acting under orders from Inspector Graham, Constable Donald Trumbley pulled his cruiser across the entrance to the Lawson laneway, blocking Steve's path.

Constable Trumbley leaned across and opened the passenger door of the cruiser. "Hop in, Truscott," he said. "We need you to verify your statement from this morning."

Steve found the officer's tone frightening. But he got in the car. Nobody told him he had rights — that he could have refused to get in alone.

• • •

Without explaining where they were headed, Constable Trumbley drove the twenty kilometres to Goderich, to the OPP detachment. There, Inspector Harold Graham awaited their arrival.

Julian Sher, in his book *Until You Are Dead,* quotes Inspector Graham boasting of this move years later to a group of police inspectors. The inspector knew that legal guidelines required a parent or social worker to be present during the interview of a child but, as Graham said, "I chose to disregard those guidelines."

Steve was handed a sheet of paper. His answers from the morning session had been typed up as though he had written the account. He was asked to read the statement out loud. He did.

"Any changes?" Graham asked.

Steve said he had not returned to the school at 8 p.m. but "a bit before 8 p.m."

The change was made. Steve signed the statement.

For another hour, Inspector Graham and Constable Trumbley took turns grilling him.

"What happened, Steve?" they asked. "Tell us the truth."

As always — as he has for more than fifty years — Steve did just that.

But the questioning went beyond details of what happened that evening. The questions became direct and accusatory.

"Have you ever taken a girl into Lawson's bush?"

"No."

"Have you ever made a date to take a girl into Lawson's bush?"

"No."

"Have you ever spoken to Jocelyne Gaudet about going into Lawson's bush?"

"No."

"Were you at Jocelyne Gaudet's house on Tuesday night?"

"No, I haven't been there since winter."

"Did you ever phone Jocelyne Gaudet?"

"No."

Inspector Graham would question Steve. He would leave the room. Constable Trumbley would enter. More questions.

The same questions.

Steve repeated his story.

Over and over.

This was no "Good Cop/Bad Cop" show. It was

more like "Bad Cop/Bad Cop." The police wanted a confession. All Steve had to do, they said, was to tell "the truth."

After ninety minutes or so — surely aware by now that his parents were searching for him — the OPP officers drove Steve back to the guardhouse at the base in Clinton. Shortly after, Steve's father arrived, visibly upset.

Surely, Steve thought, this would now end.

But the interrogation continued. The guardhouse was the home of the service police — the seat of authority in the Royal Canadian Air Force. Daniel Truscott, Steve's father, was an enlisted man, trained to obey.

The air base was run by officers.

The guardhouse was run by officers.

The police involved were seen as authorities and were regarded as officers.

But officers were also to be trusted. Soon, thought both father and son, the officers would realize he was telling the truth and Steve could go home.

At some point in the evening, Dr. David Brooks arrived. As the base doctor, Dr. Brooks had been at the Truscott house after school that day. He had tested Steve's colour vision. Perhaps someone doubted he could have seen a yellow licence plate from the bridge to the highway.

Now the question of a medical examination was suggested. Steve's father was reluctant, but at the urging of others, agreed.

Nobody asked Steve.

Dr. Joseph Addison, the Truscott family doctor, was called in from Clinton. Working together, Dr. Addison and Dr. Brooks examined Steve. They asked him to strip.

They noted a number of scratches on his arms and legs. They were described as scratches normal for an active, outdoor boy like Steve.

The doctors also noted two open, oozing sores, one on each side of Steve's penis. Each was the size of a quarter.

Dr. Addison asked, "How did you get such a sore penis?"

Steve replied: "I don't know. It has been that way for about four or five weeks." Steve added that it wasn't sore.

"Were you masturbating?" asked Dr. Addison.

"No."

"Were you out with some girl you are trying to protect?" asked the doctor.

"No."

"Did you get it cut in a knothole?"

"No."

Finally, at about 1:30 a.m., Steve sat alone, pecking away aimlessly at a typewriter. He couldn't type; he had no message. But he admired the smooth action of the typewriter keys. Two doctors, plus Inspector Graham and Constable Trumbley, waited in the next room.

Inspector Graham thought Steve was typing out a confession. They waited.

Finally, Dr. Addison said, "I'll go back in and see if I can get a story from that boy."

He entered the room and sat with Steve. While Steve talked, he took notes.

Steve repeated the story he had been telling for four days. By now, it was 2 a.m. Steve was exhausted.

Steve's father was sent home. Should he have called a lawyer? Likely. But Dan Truscott still trusted officers — including police — to be fair. Surely no fair person could believe Steve was guilty?

At about 2:30 a.m., police took Steve to Goderich to spend the night in jail.

The next morning, Steve's father turned on the radio. The lead news item was the arrest of a fourteen-year-old boy for the murder of Lynne Harper.

He sat in shock, unwilling to believe it.

8

CHAPTER EIGHT

INJUSTICE BEGINS

JULY 14, 1959

Looking back, the arrest of Steven Truscott was a travesty. But it was nothing compared to the legal dance that continued for years.

Steve's family had hired Frank Donnelly, a well-known local lawyer. Donnelly seemed to be a good choice, but he had little experience with murder trials. In those days, there weren't many lawyers with experience in that area, especially in a little town like Goderich.

Steven's first defeat in the system came two weeks after his arrest. At the age of fourteen, he was a juvenile. The law said so. But at a special hearing, a local magistrate (a lower-court judge) made a key ruling: Steven would be tried as an adult. According to law, this could be done only when "the good of the child and the interest of community demand it." It is hard to see how this was for the good of Steven.

The distinction was important. The sentence for an adult convicted of murder was death by hanging.

But during his month in the old Goderich jail, built in 1842, Donnelly kept reassuring him.

"Don't worry," Donnelly said. "You'll never go to trial. They don't have any real evidence."

Looking back, that was true — at least the part about the evidence.

The first legal step in the process was the *preliminary hearing*. At this hearing, a judge decides if the police and Crown have enough evidence for a trial.

Like most people those days, the Truscotts trusted the legal system to get things right. Donnelly undoubtedly felt the same. And Donnelly was more than a dull, small-town lawyer. Three days after the trial ended, he was appointed a judge.

The hearing began exactly one month after Steven's arrest. Donnelly was right: the evidence was all *circumstantial*. Nobody had seen Steven harm anyone; no one had seen him take Lynne Harper into the woods. Not a single clue linked Steven to the crime scene.

Fact: Lynne Harper had been murdered and sexually assaulted. Her body had been found in Lawson's woods. No one disputed that fact.

Fact: Steven Truscott gave her a ride on his bike. They left the school somewhere between 7:15 p.m. and 7:30 p.m.

Fact: Steven had two "sores" on his penis.

Police interviewed a variety of people, adults and children, who had been at the school, at the bridge, or on the road between them on that fateful evening. The stories that emerged from those interviews were often confusing. In some cases, witnesses even contradicted each other.

However, two of Steven's seventh-grade classmates had constructed stories that implicated Steven in the crime.

Jocelyne Gaudet claimed Steven had invited her to look for calves in the woods that evening. Butch George said Steven had told police he had seen Butch at the swimming hole that night. He suggested that Steven had asked him to say he had seen him there, too.

Neither Butch nor Jocelyne was known for telling the truth. Both tended to change their story with each telling.

From their interviews, the Crown had gathered a number of people who had — or hadn't — seen Steven and Lynne together on the road that night.

In charge of the preliminary hearing was Magistrate

H. E. Holmes. He was not in good health at the time. A few months later, he died of liver failure.

Even though the Crown's case was based on flimsy evidence, the magistrate didn't hesitate. At the end of the two days, he rapped his gavel on the bench and said, "Well, in my opinion the evidence is sufficient to put the accused on trial."

Steven's lifetime walk through the swamp of Canada's legal system had begun.

9

CHAPTER NINE

THE TRIAL

SEPTEMBER 16, 1959

"Hear, hear. All rise."

Judge Ronald Ferguson swept into the courtroom in his black legal robes and took his seat on the judge's bench — higher than all others in the room.

The courtroom in Goderich courthouse was packed.

The *Crown attorney*, Glenn Hays, stood before the judge. In some countries, his job is called prosecuting attorney. His job is to present the evidence collected by police.

"My Lord, I move for the trial of Steven Murray Truscott on this indictment."

Judge Ferguson said, "Place the prisoner in the prisoner's box."

Steve was ushered into the prisoner's box — an enclosed pen facing the judge. He had spent the summer in jail. He was pale and frightened. He was on trial for his life.

"Will the accused please stand?"

Steve stood.

The court clerk read the charge: "You stand indicted by the name of Steven Murray Truscott that Steven Murray Truscott, on or about the ninth day of June, 1959, at the Township of Tuckersmith, in the County of Huron, did unlawfully murder Lynne Harper, contrary to the Criminal Code of Canada. Upon this indictment how do you plead, guilty or not guilty?"

"Not guilty."

"You are appearing, Mr. Donnelly?" the judge asked.

In front of him and to his left, stood Frank Donnelly. He had spent the summer working alone in a room across the street from the courthouse.

"I am, My Lord," Donnelly replied.

The court clerk looked directly at Steven. "Are you ready for your trial?"

Steve appeared startled by the question. How could you ever be ready? But he answered simply, "Yes."

• • •

Steve had not been free since he left Lawson's farm on Friday, June 12 — three months and four days earlier.

Now, instead of starting grade eight, he faced trial as an adult. For murder.

The whole thing, he knew, was a mistake. Surely, everyone would realize that.

At the preliminary hearing, the tangle of lies and confusion from classmates and friends had stunned him. The twisting of facts. *Surely* . . .

The jurors were selected. All twelve were local men. (Donnelly told Steve's mother that women would be "too emotional.") The jurors were allowed to call home to say they would not be home until the trial was over. The technical term is *sequestered*. This meant the jury would not be allowed to talk to anyone but each other until they'd decided whether Steve was guilty or not.

At one point, Donnelly stood and asked that there be no publicity: no television, no radio news, no newspaper reports.

"Trust me," Donnelly told Steve, "you don't want the papers filled with this every day." As if that mattered. Steve would not see the newspapers in any event.

Even so, it took the lawyers and the judge half an hour to make that decision.

Criminal trials in Canada are based on the *adversarial system*. The system grew out of trial by combat. This originated in ancient Germanic law, where legal disputes could be settled with swords, lances, or other weapons. Whoever won the fight — a duel, really — was judged to be in the right. Whoever lost was usually dead. (In some cases, it was claimed that the winner was the person killed in combat, since he had been sent heaven, which was thought to be a much better place.)

This later evolved into the *jury system*. The state, called the Crown, had a lawyer to present the evidence for *conviction*. The accused, in this case Steven Truscott, had a lawyer to defend him. The judge acts as a referee to make sure that both sides act according to law. The jury must decide the innocence or guilt based solely on the facts presented in court.

The jury was sequestered to make sure that they hear only what witnesses said in court. If jurors returned home each night, they might hear gossip and rumour. The facts to be used in the decision are only those that the judge decides are legal and fair.

Public opinion in the Goderich and Clinton area was heated, and many had judged Steven guilty when he was first arrested. The police would not arrest an innocent person, would they?

The trial began, and Crown Attorney Hays got down to business.

Hays told the jury that the whole case ". . . centres

around . . . a paved road . . . a mile and a quarter immediately east of the Town of Clinton.

"The road passes, first, on the left, a set of farm buildings. And then on the right or east, Lawson's bush . . . which has a laneway going in on its north side . . . over some railway tracks and then over a bridge . . . and then on to number eight provincial highway."

He had just described Steve's childhood playground. This was the road down which he had biked countless times. The bridge where he fished and swam. Lawson's woods, where he and Leslie Spilsbury had built a tree fort, and found a cow and calf that they had brought back to Bob Lawson.

The Crown attorney kept talking.

"One of the things you may find . . . of very considerable significance, were some — an item of the clothing of the accused, taken from him some time after his arrest."

Steve winced. That would be the underwear they had taken from him in jail. Alone, in jail that first night, frightened, he had crapped himself. The next day, they had ordered him to strip and had taken his clothes. Was they what they were talking about?

In his opening statement to the jury, Crown Attorney Hays rambled through a list of the *testimony* the jury would hear.

Then he strayed into swampy legal territory by referring to the statement that Steven had signed on the night of his arrest:

". . . a statement was taken from the accused by Inspector Graham and the other police, one of the other policemen, signed that night by him . . ."

Immediately, the judge jumped all over the Crown attorney.

"Mr. Hays," the judge said, sternly, looking down from the bench like a teacher handing out a detention.

Crown Attorney Hays looked like a little boy with a hand in the cookie jar. "I didn't intend to say anything about it," Hays said.

Simply by mentioning Steven had signed a statement, Hays had stepped over a legal line. Without knowing the contents of the statement, the jury might conclude that Steven had confessed. Thus, once Hays said a statement had been made, it had to be introduced in court so the jury could see the contents.

The judge replied, "You should not have said *anything* about it at all."

"Even the fact that it was taken at all?" asked Hays.

The judge got red in the face. "I may have to discharge the jury and start over again. You shouldn't do that, you know. I will have to consider that."

The jury was sent from the room. Legal arguments followed. Finally, the judge said, "If the statement is not admitted, you have made a mistrial, Mr. Hays. If it is admitted, there is no harm done, of course. That is the position."

The statement itself said only that Steven had given Lynne Harper a ride to the highway and let her off — exactly what Steven had been saying for months. But the jury would never know that.

The statement never was admitted.

If you believed the judge, a mistrial was in order. That never happened.

Even the Supreme Court, months later, ruled that no mistrial had taken place. They stated that by not forcing this issue, the defence had missed its only chance for a mistrial. They would have to start all over again.

• • •

The case the Crown tried to prove at the trial — and persisted with for forty-seven years — was simple: Steven Truscott gave Lynne Harper a ride on his bike. They left the school and proceeded down the county road.

But when Steve and Lynne got as far as the "tractor trail" into Lawson's bush, the Crown alleged, Steven took Lynne into the woods, sexually assaulted her, strangled her with her blouse, and tried to cover her body with tree branches.

According to this story, Steven then got back on his bicycle, returned to the school shortly before eight o'clock, and acted as though nothing had happened.

Including the time it takes to bicycle to and from the woods, he did all this in forty-five minutes or less. He did it without breaking into a sweat, on an evening when the temperature was a sultry thirty degrees Celsius.

Clearly, the time of death was key to the Crown's story. Which is why the court battle between medical experts mattered so much.

The key Crown witness was Dr. Penistan, the pathologist. He had been called to see Lynne's body in the woods.

Dr. Penistan had repeated — more or less — details from the autopsy. Lynne Harper had been sexually assaulted. She had been strangled with her own blouse. In his opinion, the doctor said, the crime had been committed in the woods where the body was found.

Without hesitation, Dr. Penistan told the court that Lynne Harper had died between 7 p.m. and 7:45 p.m.

This, of course, was exactly the time during which Steven said he was with Lynne, and to the jury must have appeared very incriminating. If true, this was the strongest link between Steven and the murder.

However, later in the trial, the defence lawyer produced an expert who said this time accuracy was almost impossible. Dr. Berkeley Brown taught at the University of Western Ontario medical school and specialized in the digestive system. He testified that the stomach normally empties between three and a half and four hours after a meal — and even that can be delayed if the meal was not well chewed.

At the time of the trial, the jury had to make a choice. Whom should they believe: an expert in the field who taught doctors in training at a university? Or a country pathologist from a small town who based his estimate on when he was told Lynne Harper had eaten? (One jury member said later that he believed Dr. Penistan because he didn't have to refer to his notes.)

One other fact that would not emerge for almost half a century: six years after the trial, Dr. Penistan himself changed his mind. In a special report, he wrote that Lynne could have died as much as several hours later.

But in 1959, with a fourteen-year-old boy's life at stake, he had no doubts.

Dr. Penistan drew some exact conclusions. "The food in the stomach appeared to have been very poorly chewed," Dr. Penistan told the jury. "[It] appeared to have been bolted, and swallowed without proper chewing."

And finally: "I . . . make some allowance for the fact of the poor chewing of the food and give as my opinion that the food had not been in the stomach for more than two hours."

"Could it have been for a lesser time?" asked the Crown attorney.

"It could certainly, sir, have been for a lesser time."

"To what?"

"I would estimate between one and two hours."

"You were in the courtroom when Mrs. Harper testified this girl finished her meal at a quarter to six?"

"I was, sir."

"On that basis, sir, you would put her time of death at . . . ?"

"As prior to a quarter to eight."

"As early as . . . ?" prompted the Crown attorney.

"Probably between seven and a quarter to eight," Dr. Penistan said firmly. Exactly the time period that the Crown could easily show Steven was with her.

10

CHAPTER TEN

JOCELYNE GAUDET

SEPTEMBER 17, 1959

Jocelyne Gaudet was a pretty thirteen-year-old with hair in ringlets. She was the first of the children to testify.

She snuggled into the witness stand at the trial. She looked up fleetingly and locked eyes with Steven. Quickly, they both looked elsewhere.

With Jocelyne on the witness stand, Steve felt anger rise in him. He could understand why police had questioned Lynne's classmates. Everyone had done what they could to help when Lynne went missing. What he could not understand was why the police had twisted those words to make him look guilty. What baffled him even more was why Jocelyne had lied.

In July, at the preliminary hearing, her lies were crucial to the decision to put Steven on trial. Now, however, her lies could be a matter of life and death. Steven's life.

Surely this time she would see this was serious and stop lying. Wouldn't she?

Jocelyne smirked and tossed her head and would not look at him again.

The judge leaned forward in the bench. "How old are you?" he asked Jocelyne.

"Thirteen."

"Do you go to school?"

"Yes, sir."

"What grade are you in?"

"Grade eight," Jocelyne answered.

Judge Ferguson looked over his glasses at the girl. "Well, what does it mean to take an oath?"

Jocelyne looked flushed. "Well, you are not supposed to tell lies."

The judge looked relieved. He straightened up. "You understand that, do you?"

Jocelyne nodded.

"I think she is old enough to be sworn," said the judge.

The registrar held a Bible out to Jocelyne. "Place your right hand on the Bible."

Jocelyne did so.

"Do you swear to tell the truth, the whole truth, and nothing but the truth, so help you God?"

"I do."

The clerk retreated. Crown Attorney Hays rose to his feet.

"Jocelyne, last spring were you in the same grade, seven, at the school, as Lynne Harper and Steven Truscott?"

"Yes, sir."

"And on Monday, June 8, Jocelyne, did you have a conversation at school with Steve Truscott?"

"Yes, sir."

"Will you tell what that conversation was, please?"

"Well, on Sunday, I had gone to Bob Lawson's barn and I had seen a calf there. I mentioned that to Steve on Monday, and he asked me if I wanted to see two more newborn calves."

"Go on, please."

"And I said 'Yes,' and he asked me if I could make it on Monday and I said 'No,' because I had to go to Guides."

"Make what?" asked Hays.

"If I could go with him to see the calves and I said 'No,' and then he asked me if I could make it on Tuesday and I said I would try. On Tuesday, he told me if I could go and I just told him I didn't know."

She paused. The courtroom fell silent.

"And he said to meet him on the right-hand side of the county road, just outside the fence by the woods. He kept telling me not tell anybody because Bob didn't like a whole bunch of kids on his property."

The meeting place she described was where the county road met the tractor trail — only ninety metres or so from where Lynne's body was found.

"I got out of the house about twenty after six or six-thirty, and then I went towards over to Bob Lawson's barn, and I asked him . . ."

Crown Attorney Hays interrupted: "No. What did you go to Bob Lawson's barn for?"

"To see if Steve was there."

"And after you left [the barn] where did you go?" asked Hays.

"To see if Steve was at the meeting place."

"I take it you didn't see Steve."

"No."

"And then where did you go?"

Jocelyne replied: "I went towards the river. I just bicycled. I saw Philip Burns."

"And where did you go then?"

"There is a sort of a trailer or tractor road or something, and I turned down that and went three-quarters of the way in. I looked toward the railroad bridge and

I shouted Steve's name twice. Then I looked toward the woods, and shouted it three or four times. When I looked up, I saw Arnold George going past."

"And then what did you do?" asked Hays.

"I got out of the lane and then I went down towards the river."

"What did you go down there for, Jocelyne?"

"I just went down to see if Steve would be at the river," Jocelyne replied.

"And was he?"

"Well, I didn't see him."

"And what did you do after that?"

"I stayed there for five or ten minutes and then I went back to Bob's farm."

"Did you see Steve anytime that night?"

"No."

"Did you see Lynne Harper anytime that night?"

"Not after five o'clock, I didn't."

A few minutes later, Crown Attorney Hays asked Jocelyne what time she returned to Bob Lawson's barn.

"A little before seven."

"How long did you stay there?"

"About an hour and a half."

• • •

After Jocelyne's testimony, Donnelly cross-examined her in particular about the two visits to Lawson's barn that evening. In doing so, he failed to point out the time discrepancies in her story — she was out by thirty to forty minutes.

"What was he doing when you got there first?"

"He was feeding the pigs."

"And when you came back, what was he doing?"

"I didn't notice. I just went in and talked to him."

"What was he doing?"

"Work," Jocelyne replied.

"What kind of work?"

"He let the cows out of the barn and then he cleaned the barn a little and fed the calf and did jobs like that."

"And you stayed for an hour and a half?"

"About that."

"And you were back at Lawson's some time before seven o'clock? Ten to seven?"

"Yes, sir."

Donnelly might have deflated her story if he had known that in her first statement, Jocelyne said she had been looking for Lynne Harper. On June 12, she told Constable Trumbley that she had walked with her bicycle along the tractor trail "to the corner where the bush extends to the north again" — about 200 metres from the road. At the preliminary hearing she altered this, saying, "The police — they had a stake there where the bicycle marks were. I went about that far and then I turned my bicycle and went up the county road again." By the trial, this was amended again: "I turned down [the tractor trail] and went three-quarters of the way in."

In only a few days, she had made three different statements to police and seemed to have no trouble adjusting her story from time to time.

Steve was angry — Jocelyne's story was meaningless. If Jocelyne was back at Lawson's barn before 7 p.m., of course she would not have seen him. He didn't meet Lynne until after 7 p.m., and they didn't leave the school until almost 7:30 p.m.

He hoped the jury would see the confusion in the lies.

11

CHAPTER ELEVEN

ARNOLD "BUTCH" GEORGE

SEPTEMBER 17, 1959

Butch George had been one of Steve's best friends. But his testimony at the preliminary hearing in July had been damning — and enough to send the case to trial.

As Butch came to the stand, Steve wondered: would his story be the same? Butch had a history of making things up. Whatever story you want to hear, Butch could usually provide it. That was good when fooling around with the guys. But not in a courtroom.

At the preliminary trial in July, Butch had seemed to remember bits of one conversation and bits of another. Then he had patched them together to form a new story.

Butch took his place in the witness box and was sworn in — but not before he startled the judge.

"Do you know what happens to people when they don't tell the truth?" asked Judge Ferguson.

"My dad told me something about that and I forget now."

Judge Ferguson sat upright.

"You forget." The judge looked puzzled. He turned to Crown Attorney Hays. "All right. Do you want this boy sworn, Mr. Hays?"

"If Your Lordship feels . . ."

"It is important whether they are sworn or not. He doesn't seem to appreciate quite the nature of an oath and what the consequences are."

Hays was now in a bind. A sworn witness could be believed. An unsworn witness could only support testimony from a sworn witness. It was an important difference.

"I would like to see him sworn, My Lord, if he can be, but it is discretionary."

Now the judge had a decision to make. He looked down at Butch.

"Do you go to church, young man?"

"Well, not regularly."

The judge sighed impatiently. He turned to the court registrar. "Age thirteen, he should be able to understand these things. I think you better swear him."

• • •

After some preliminary questions, Crown Attorney

Hays asked Butch about his meeting with Jocelyne that evening. He had been biking north on the county road to the swimming hole when he saw Jocelyne on the tractor trail.

"And you did meet Jocelyne Gaudet near where?" asked Hays.

"The side of the woods," Butch replied. "The side nearest the river."

"Where was she?"

"She was about forty feet from the road . . . back in towards the bush there, on the lane."

"Which direction was she going?"

"Towards me."

"And what time do you say this was, Arnold, that you met Jocelyne there?"

Butch replied, "About twenty minutes after seven."

But Jocelyne had said she had returned to the Lawson barn about ten minutes *before* 7 o'clock. Their times were out by half an hour.

"And where did you go from there?"

"I cut down along the river there, to the swimming hole, and I went swimming with these boys. Well, first of all, I stopped — Jocelyne shouted back to me and she said —"

The judge stopped Butch. Court rules did not allow

witnesses to repeat what others had said. Witnesses could state only what they themselves had asked or said, unless the conversation took place with the accused present — in this case, Steven.

"Where was Jocelyne at that time?" asked Hays.

"She was up at the parking lot, about where the parking lot is."

"Was she on foot or on bicycle?"

Butch paused for a moment. "It is hard to tell. I didn't notice her. Like, I just heard her and I looked back and she asked me if I had seen Steve."

Butch said he had stayed at the swimming hole until about 8:30 p.m. and then went home. At no time did he see Lynne Harper that evening. Once he got home, however, he left to see Steve.

Hays asked: "You went down to Steve's place?"

"Yes."

Steve made fists of his hands and held on tight. He was lying. Butch was lying.

"What time was that?"

"That was about a quarter to nine."

"And did you have a conversation with him?"

"I asked him where he had been that night and he said: 'Down at the river.' I said: 'I heard that you had given Lynne a ride down to the river,' and he said: 'Yes, she wanted a lift down to number eight highway.'

"And I said: 'I heard you were in the bush with her,' and he said: 'No, we were on the side of the bush looking for a cow and calf.' And he said: 'Why do you want to know for?' and I said: 'Skip it and let' s play ball.'"

Lies, lies, lies. Steve pressed his lips together. Butch would not look at him.

A few minutes later, Butch remembered another conversation.

"When was that?" asked Hays.

"It was in the evening, I think."

"Wednesday, June 10, then?"

"Mmhmmm."

"That 'Mmmhmmm' means yes, does it?"

"Yes," said Butch.

"And what was said on that occasion?"

Butch didn't seem to know where to look. "Well, he said that the police had questioned him . . . and that he had told them he had seen me," Butch said. "[But] it wasn't me, it was Gordie Logan. He thought that Gordie was me so he told the police that.

"He said that the police were going to go down to my place to check up, so I agreed that I would tell them I had seen Steve."

In other words, Butch said, he had agreed to lie to

the police because Steve had asked him to. Whatever the cause of this confusion, it made Steven look guilty.

Butch also said he and Steve had joined several others on the bridge on June 10. That was the day after Lynne went missing, and the day before her body was found.

About that conversation, Hays asked, "Now, what was said, Arnold?"

"Well, Paul [Desjardine] said to Steve: 'I heard you had Lynne up in the bush with you.' And he said: 'No, I didn't, did I, Butch?' And I said: 'No, he had her at the side of the bush.'"

"Repeat that?"

"'You had her at the side of the bush looking for the cow and the calf.'"

"Who said that?"

"Me."

• • •

When Frank Donnelly rose to begin his cross-examination of Butch George, he had what should have been an easy job: to show that Butch's word was not reliable.

Donnelly asked Butch to think back to the evening when Lynne was last seen. Had he been looking for Steve? Donnelly asked.

"Yes."

"At any time, from the time you started to look for

him until you found him at his home at nine o'clock that evening, did you see him anywhere?"

"No, sir."

"Did you see his bicycle anywhere?"

Steve's bicycle was unique: an English three-speed racing bike with ten-colour tassels, each almost a foot long, attached to each handle. It would be hard to miss.

"No."

"And if this bicycle had been laying [*sic*] along the road, along Lawson's bush . . . you would have seen it, wouldn't you?"

"Yes."

"And when you stopped to talk to Jocelyne Gaudet, were you about opposite the laneway running along the north side of the bush?"

"Yes."

"And she was in, you said, about forty feet?"

"Yes."

"And could you see along the north side of the bush for some distance?"

"Yes."

"And did you see that bicycle lying alongside of the north side of the bush?"

"No."

Donnelly did challenge Butch on the conflict with

his testimony at the preliminary hearing. He read from the transcript of that hearing. Butch had then described his meeting at Steve's house on June 9 but had not mentioned the story of the cow and calf.

"Those answers were true?" he asked.

"Yes," replied Butch.

Donnelly straightened up, the transcript still in his hand. He looked over his glasses at the boy. "And at that time . . . you said nothing about Truscott having mentioned of being at the side of the bush looking for a cow and calf. I suggest that wasn't said on that occasion at all. If it was said at any time at all, it was down at the bridge?"

"He said it that night, when I was up at his house." But Butch didn't sound quite sure. Steve gripped his chair. Butch was lying. He had never come to the house that night.

"Why didn't you tell us that? You told us in July what he said, and you didn't tell us that then?"

"I forgot."

It was a great feat of forgetting. Years later, Butch's statements to police would reveal what police and the Crown knew at the trial: that Butch had offered the story about Steve taking Lynne Harper to look for calves *before anyone knew Lynne was missing.* Shortly after Butch returned from the swimming hole, he had told friends that Steve had taken Lynne into the woods. At the same time, he admitted he had not witnessed this, and at the time had neither seen nor talked to Steve.

Donnelly didn't know that, but even so he pressed to clarify. "Your memory would be a whole lot better two months ago than it would be today, wouldn't it?"

"Well, I stated that statement while I was — during that time."

Usually lawyers never ask questions to which they don't know the answer. This avoids unexpected answers. But now, Donnelly sensed an opening.

Had the police provided information that improved his memory? Donnelly asked.

Finally, Butch said, "Well, they, like, parts of my statement had been lost and they gave me another sheet."

"When?"

"Two weeks ago."

Steve glared at his former friend.

Donnelly continued. "And how often did you read that over before you came to court?"

"About ten times."

"Ten times. You memorized the sheet that was given to you, did you?"

"I wasn't trying to memorize it."

"Why were you going over it so often?"

"Trying to make sure what I said, what I was going to say."

Finally, Donnelly tried to clarify. "You never did see Steve at the side of the woods, did you?"

"No."

"And you don't know whether Steve saw you down at the river or not, do you?"

Butch didn't answer.

"Now, how many statements did you give to police?"

"Three."

"And they were all different, weren't they?"

"The first two were."

"So you gave three statements?"

"Yes."

"And they were all different?"

"Yes."

"Was this sheet that was given to you two weeks ago from the first, second, or third statement?"

"The third."

Before he left the witness stand, Butch George appeared confused about whether he had talked to police or his friends first on Wednesday night or Tuesday night. Even so, one statement must have stuck with the jury:

"When the body was found," he said, "I changed my story."

Steve with his racing bike a few weeks
before Lynne's murder. Note the tassels
hanging from the handlegrips.

Lynne Harper, age 12.

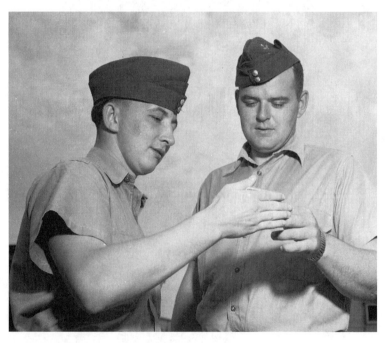

Corporal George Edens and Lieutenant Joseph Leger were the searchers who discovered Lynne's body.

Tractor trail beside Bob Lawson's bush. Lynne's body is being carried away, June 11, 1959.

Police near where Lynne's body was found, June 11, 1959. One officer is carrying branches that covered Lynne's body. The other is carrying jackets, possibly those used to cover her body by searchers.

An unidentified member of the air force search party on the site where the body was found. The stakes mark the position of the body.

Dr. John Penistan, the coroner, exits a car on the county road as he arrived at the crime scene.

Inspector Harold Graham of the OPP Criminal Investigations Branch arrives at the air force base a few hours after the body was found.

Lynne Harper's funeral, the day after Steve was arrested.

Steve is taken to the courthouse in Goderich, June 18, 1959.

Steve being taken away by police.

Steve Truscott while in youth detention, 1966, around the time of his Supreme Court Review, Guelph, Ontario

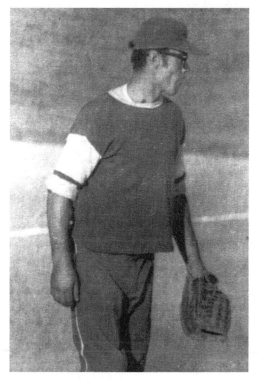

Steve played third base on the Collins Bay baseball team. This picture was taken only weeks before Steve was granted parole.

12

CHAPTER TWELVE

DOUGIE OATES AND THE TURTLES

SEPTEMBER 27, 1959

When it came time for Steven's lawyer to present the defence arguments, the job may have seemed easy. In spite of the parade of sixty-one witnesses for the prosecution, the case was all circumstantial. No hard evidence existed.

In theory, all the defence had to do was produce one solid witness who saw Steve and Lynne cross the bridge, just as Steve said had happened.

Just one such witness would cripple the Crown's case. Three would remove all doubt.

If Frank Donnelly appeared confident when he started his presentation of the defence, it may have been because he had three such witnesses. (A fourth witness existed, but that fact lay hidden for forty years.)

First up was Dougie Oates, a gritty twelve-year-old nature lover.

For the trial, he had travelled from his new home in Trenton, Ontario. It was a long trip: 355 kilometres, and only portions through Toronto were on the new expressway, Highway 401. It took eight hours. His father, also in the RCAF, had been transferred from Clinton to the base at Trenton.

Dougie sat in the witness stand. Judge Ferguson looked down at him. "Do you understand what it means to take an oath in a courtroom?"

"Yes, sir."

"What does it mean?"

Dougie did not hesitate. "It means you are calling on God to watch you, and if you don't tell the truth then you are committing a sin."

Judge Ferguson leaned back in his chair. It was not clear to those in the courtroom what system he used in judging young people.

"I don't think I should swear a boy of this age. Do you want this boy sworn, Mr. Donnelly?"

Donnelly paused. He shuffled some papers.

"This witness might give some very important evidence . . . I would like to see the witness sworn if Your Lordship thinks he should be sworn."

The judge paused, thoughtfully.

"I think we will swear him. The boy seems pretty

intelligent and seems to understand the obligation to tell the truth."

Dougie wriggled into the chair. He was prepared for a long session.

In response to Donnelly's questions, he told the court about going down to the bridge on the county road that night — the night Lynne Harper disappeared. He had been hunting turtles.

"Did you see any?" Donnelly asked.

"Yes, two of them . . . I was going to go in to get the first one and Ronnie told me to stay up on the bridge. He took his fishing rod and snagged the turtle by the leg and brought it up and put it in the carrier." That would be Ronnie Demaray.

"What carrier?"

"Karen Daum' s carrier." Karen Daum was the younger sister of one of Dougie's friends.

"A bicycle carrier?"

"Yes."

"And then?"

Dougie continued. "He started to get ready to go home and I saw one more turtle, it was quite small, and I went down and watched it go down, and then I went down to the bottom of the bridge and grabbed it."

"You grabbed the turtle?"

"Yes, sir."

"What did you do then?"

"Well, then, I took it up to the top of the bridge and when Ronnie saw it, he wanted — he asked me for it and he gave me the two bigger turtles."

"And then?"

"He put it in a bag and went home."

Dougie Oates had provided a clear picture of a very ordinary evening in the life of ordinary kid: one small turtle in an even trade for two bigger turtles.

Donnelly then turned to more serious business.

"At any time that evening did you see Steve Truscott and Lynne Harper?"

"Yes, sir."

"Where?"

"Came by me on the bridge," Dougie replied.

"What were you doing on the bridge at that time?"

Dougie glanced at the jury and continued. He knew that what he had seen was important. "When they were coming by, I turned around and put up my hand and said, 'Hi.'"

"You put up your hand and said 'Hi'?"

"Yes, sir."

"How were they travelling?"

"They were riding double on their bike."

"Did you know the bicycle?"

"No, sir."

"Who was pedalling?"

"Steve was pedalling."

"How was Lynne sitting?"

"She was sitting on the crossbar, sir . . . facing east, towards Seaforth," Dougie said.

"On which side of the bridge were you?"

"I was on the east side."

"So you put up your hand and you said, 'Hi,' and what did Lynne do?"

"She smiled."

"What did Steve do?"

Dougie glanced at Steve in the prisoner's box. Steve didn't look up. "I don't think he noticed me because he just kept on riding down."

"Which way were they going at that time?"

"They were going north, towards the highway, number eight highway."

"Which direction were they from the bridge at that time?"

"They were on the north of the bridge."

"North of the bridge?"

"Yes, sir. They were going north on the east side, sir."

After a few more questions, Donnelly wrapped up.

He asked Dougie to point out where Steve and Lynne were when he saw them. Pointing to a map, he indicated the north end of the bridge over the Bayfield River.

"Did you ever see Lynne again?" asked Donnelly.

"No, I didn't, sir."

"Did you ever see Steve again?"

"Yes, sir . . . About three days later."

"You didn't see him again that night?"

"No, sir."

"How long did you stay at the bridge?"

"I was there around until about seven-thirty, because I got home at fifteen to eight."

"You got home —"

"At fifteen minutes to eight."

Donnelly looked up and gazed at the jury. To make sure they had not missed the point, he repeated, "Fifteen minutes to eight?"

"Yes, sir."

Donnelly now turned to the Crown attorney. "Your witness, Mr. Hays," he said, and returned to his seat.

• • •

Crown Attorney Hays rose and looked at Dougie Oates, twelve years old, one hundred and five pounds. Hays knew he had to move in quickly to challenge the young witness. If the jury believed Dougie, the Crown case did not stand up. It should be no contest: an educated, articulate, experienced, and polished lawyer against an urchin.

"Where did you see Steve three days later?" he asked, referring to a question Dougie had answered a few minutes before. The aim was to throw him off, to appear confused. It didn't work.

"Down beside McLaren's house, near the woods, on the station."

"And what did he say to you?

"I wasn't talking to him, sir."

Now the Crown attorney closed in, almost mocking in tone.

"You have never talked to Steve since this evening?"

"I said 'Hi' to him once more."

"Pardon?" said the Crown attorney, almost in disbelief.

"I said 'Hi' to him once more, and that was the last thing I said to him."

"Did you never talk to him about seeing him that night?"

"No, sir."

"Did you only see him once that night?"

"Yes, sir."

"And what time do you say that was?"

"I couldn't recall."

"You don't know what time?"

"No, sir."

Now, thought the Crown attorney, and he moved to deflate Dougie's story. "Well now, other witnesses have told us of seeing Steve down there by himself at six-thirty, Douglas. Is there a chance that that is what you saw?"

"No, it isn't, sir."

"And then you have added Lynne, through anything else you heard after?"

"Pardon?"

"Did you simply add Lynne through things you heard after?"

"No, I saw him and Lynne."

"Can you assist us as to what time it was you saw them?"

"No, I couldn't."

"Well, would you disagree with me that it was about six-thirty?"

"Yes, I would."

"What time do you say it would be that you saw him?"

"I couldn't say. I know it wouldn't be six-thirty."

"Well, would it be before seven?"

"No, sir."

"Are you sure it was after seven?"

"Yes, sir."

Crown Attorney Hays reached into a pile of papers on the desk. "Do you remember giving the police a statement on the Saturday, that is, the thirteenth of June?"

"I remember giving them one."

"What did you say about the time, that time?"

"I can't remember."

"What time did you tell them it was that you saw this?"

"I think it was some time after seven."

Hays now held out the paper he had taken from his desk. "I suggest to you that you said it might have been seven o'clock." He began to read: "'*I don't know the time, but I think half an hour either way from seven o'clock.*' Did you tell them that?" He waved the paper in front of Dougie's eyes as though he had caught the boy in a lie.

"Well, I didn't say it was half an hour either way. I said it could have been half an hour after seven."

"You didn't tell them it could be half an hour either way?"

"No, I didn't."

"You said it could have been seven or half an hour later; is that what you say?"

"Yes."

Crown Attorney Hays waved the paper — the statement given to police. "Constable Trumbley read the statement back to you, but you wouldn't sign it. Is that so?"

"He didn't read it back to me. He gave it to me to read and I never got finished reading it, though, and I didn't sign it because mother said not to sign it unless she read it first."

"Did you finish reading it, yourself?"

"No, sir."

"Why?"

"He didn't give me enough time, sir."

Hays handed the paper to Dougie Oates.

"Read it over," he said.

Judge Ferguson intervened. "We will have to have a recess to read it over."

Hays pulled the paper back from the boy. "May I read it to him, My Lord?"

With a nod for approval, the Crown attorney began to read.

> *I am 11 years old and in Grade 5 at AVMC*
> *School. Lynne was missing on Tuesday night*
> *June 9th. I had supper, starting at about 5*
> *o'clock, and after supper about 5:30 I did the*
> *dishes and left the house about 6 o'clock. I*

then called for Rodney Dam [sic], but he was gone to the river, and I left his place and rode on my bicycle down the country road to the car bridge. It would just take about five minutes for me to get down there.

I saw the oldest Demaray boy sitting fishing down under the bridge. I talked to him and he caught a turtle, and then when he finished fishing I went in after a turtle, and then he left from just there and Karen Daum came up. I don't know who else was fishing, but Karen and I looked for turtles for a while, maybe fifteen minutes, then we were fixing our bike carriers up so the turtles couldn't get away, so we could put them in there and not have to carry them and ride our bikes one-handed.

Before Karen came up I saw Steve and Lynne ride by, they were riding double on Steve's bike, going towards the highway. I saw them at the bridge before Karen Daum came up, it might have been about 7 o'clock. I don't know the time but I think a half hour either way from 7 o'clock.

I was under the bridge once in a while, but when I saw them go by I was on top of the bridge. I didn't see either Steve or Lynne again that night. I don't think I could say what they were wearing. I didn't look at the clock when I got home, but I am supposed to be home around 8 o'clock. I understand what taking an oath means in Court.

Hays looked up. "Now, did you tell the police that?"

"Not all of that, sir. I didn't say that I saw — I saw them at seven o'clock either way."

"What did you say?"

"I said that I saw them at seven o'clock or after seven."

The time element was crucial to the Crown's case. Hays repeatedly tried to shake his little witness. Finally, he threw up his hands in desperation.

"Oh, I see. What makes you so sure it couldn't be before seven o'clock, Douglas?"

"Because I was down there for about an hour looking at the turtles."

"How do you know it was an hour?"

"I couldn't have seen them until about seven anyway because I was looking for the turtles for about fifteen minutes."

"Why do you say fifteen minutes, Douglas?"

"Because time goes by quite fast when you are doing something."

Still trying to rush the witness into stretching time to better fit the Crown case, Hays continued:

"Did you go home on your bike?"

"Yes."

"How long would that be after you say you saw Steve and Lynne go by on their bike?"

"I couldn't answer that neither, sir."

"Well, would it be an hour afterwards or what would it be?"

"I don't think it would be an hour."

But Hays continued to press. Dougie pushed back, insisting that after Steve and Lynne had gone by, he and Karen had put the turtles in the carrier and gone home.

"We were just looking for a couple of more turtles and we fixed up the carrier."

"How long do you think you looked?"

"Maybe about ten to fifteen minutes."

Hays blew a breath toward the ceiling. "Ten to fifteen minutes. Do you think it would be that long for you to look and put your turtles in the carrier?"

But never rush a patient hunter. Dougie Oates replied, "Yes, because we were letting them crawl along the ground."

Snickers in the courtroom.

"And then you went directly home?"

"We stopped at the railroad tracks."

"How long?"

"For about ten minutes, because there was a turtle there had been run over by cars quite a few times, because it was pretty well dried out, and I took off the claws and put them in my top pocket of my shirt and went home."

More snickers.

"You got home at what time?"

"About fifteen to eight."

Shortly after this, Crown Attorney Hays sat down. How do you defeat a witness who trades in racing turtles and collects their claws in a shirt pocket?

13

CHAPTER THIRTEEN

PROOF OF INNOCENCE

SEPTEMBER 18, 1959

Gordon Logan was thirteen, in grade seven, and a friend of Steve's. On the evening of June 9, he told the court, his evening had been about fishing and swimming.

Gordon spoke of meeting another classmate that evening, Richard Gellatly, who gave him a ride on his bike down to the car bridge (about 1,500 metres away).

There, Gord had gone to the swimming hole 200 metres east of the bridge, and Richard had gone home to get his bathing suit.

"And then . . . ?" asked Donnelly.

"I went in swimming for about — until about seven-thirty, and then I saw Steve and Lynne go by the bridge on Steve's bicycle."

"You say you saw Steve and Lynne go across the

bridge?" repeated Donnelly. He couldn't risk the jury missing this key fact.

"How were they travelling?

"They were riding double on Steve's bicycle . . . [Lynne was] sitting on the crossbar."

"Did you see either of them again?"

Gord testified that he saw Steve return alone about five minutes later. "I saw Steve ride back to the bridge and I saw him stop at the bridge."

Donnelly felt confident at this point. With a testimony by Dougie Oates's older brother, Alan, who testified he had seen Steven at the bridge after 7:30 p.m., he had now presented three witnesses who supported Steve's story.

When it came time for cross-examination, Crown Attorney Hays worked hard at planting seeds of doubt in the minds of the jury. He had to counter the three witnesses who supported Steven's story. The gloves came off.

"I suggest to you, Gordon," said Hays, "that standing where you say you were standing, that you could not tell anyone on that bridge. That you couldn't tell a boy from a man or a girl from a woman."

"I disagree."

Even Judge Ferguson joined in the fray.

"Is the rock not six hundred feet east of the road bridge?" asked the judge.

"No sir, I don't think it is."

"How far do you think it is?"

"Three hundred."

"That is one hundred yards," mused the judge. (About one hundred metres.)

If doubts about Gord's eyesight from the judge were not enough, Hays later brought back Constable Trumbley of the OPP to testify that he couldn't make out features of a person from that distance.

No one ever thought to test Gord Logan to see if *he* could identify a boy and girl on a bike while standing on that rock.

Years later, police tests confirmed that you could.

Even worse, everyone ignored the fact that from the same distance, Crown witnesses Jocelyne Gaudet and Butch George had recognized each other. Butch was in the swimming hole and Jocelyne in the parking lot up the road near the tracks. They apparently not only recognized each other, but talked across the distance.

14

CHAPTER FOURTEEN

THE DEFENCE RESTS

SEPTEMBER 30, 1959

When Frank Donnelly rose to give his closing arguments to the jury, the trial had been going on for one day short of two weeks.

The jury had been sequestered — isolated — all that time. They had eaten together, rested together, and had been prisoners themselves for that time. They had not been allowed to phone home.

They were not in a good mood.

And they were now to be bombarded with two full days of summing up — by the defence, by the Crown, and then instructions to the jury by the judge. If you've ever sat through a lecture lasting more than one full hour, you may have some idea of how they felt.

Frank Donnelly had little more to add, but he took a full day in court to add it.

He began: "Now, in this particular trial we have what is known as direct evidence and circumstantial evidence."

The jury slumped in their seats. Two weeks of sitting through seventy-one witnesses and now this? A lecture from law school?

Donnelly droned on: "Now, there is direct evidence that this young girl was murdered. You have heard the evidence of the three members of the air force who found the body. You have heard Dr. Penistan and . . . this girl was murdered. That is direct evidence.

"But there is no direct evidence which in any way links this boy with that murder."

Which was true.

In essence, though, Crown Attorney Hays had been right in his opening statement. The whole case came down to that one hour period on the night of June 9, on a 1.6-kilometre section of the county road north from the air base to Highway 8. That road ran first past Lawson's woods and then over the bridge.

In the summation, both the Crown and the defence focused on the testimony of two witnesses: Richard Gellatly and Philip Burns, both of whom had left the bridge at the same time and proceeded along the county road south to the air base.

Richard had left the south end of the bridge at about

7:20 p.m., riding his bike. Philip Burns, age ten, had left about the same time, on foot. Oddly, neither remember seeing each other, but an adult witness placed both on the county road near the bridge about that time. Richard rode his bike to the school on the county road and met Lynne and Steven near O'Brien's farm (about 250 metres from the school). Philip, walking the same route, did not see Steven and Lynne.

Philip had not mentioned seeing Jocelyne Gaudet and Butch George, nor any one of several other people on the road at the time, including Steve and Lynne.

Donnelly simply noted that Philip was an unsworn witness. The jury cannot use the testimony of an unsworn witness to convict or acquit someone.

Crown Attorney Hays wove the story more convincingly. "But Philip Burns," Hays insisted, "testifies that he did not meet Steve and Lynne or either of them."

He stopped and looked directly at the jury.

"I ask you, is that not pretty conclusive that Steve and Lynne turned off the county road into the bush? What other explanation is there? Where else could they have gone?"

Where indeed?

The Crown attorney didn't bother to mention that Philip Burns was an unsworn witness, or that the defence had three sworn witnesses who placed Steven at the bridge when he said he had been at the bridge: Dougie Oates, Gord Logan, and Alan Oates.

Hays had a different view of this same information. His whole summation supported the story the Crown wanted the jury to believe: that Steven had taken Lynne Harper into Lawson's woods, strangled and raped her, covered her body with branches from saplings growing nearby, and returned to the schoolyard.

Witnesses who said they saw Steve and Lynne cross the Bayfield bridge, he called liars: Dougie Oates was a liar, Gord Logan was a liar, Alan Oates was a liar, each sticking up for a friend.

At what should have been the end of thirteen days of trial, the defence basically said: the evidence is all circumstantial and we have witnesses who support Steven's story. The Crown simply called them all liars and said only Steven could have committed this crime.

Then the judge gave his instructions to the jury.

15

CHAPTER FIFTEEN

HERE COMES THE JUDGE

SEPTEMBER 30, 1959

After eleven days of trial (thirteen days, with Sundays off) the jury had spent one whole day listening to the defence sum up. Six unstoppable hours. They then spent a whole day listening to Crown Attorney Glenn Hays summing up.

By then, it was 4:30 p.m. on the — lucky? — thirteenth day of the trial. The jury was tired at this point: tired of testimony, tired of the courtroom, tired of droning voices that often repeated the same points.

Instead of letting the jury go and resuming the following day, Judge Ferguson gave everyone a fifteen-minute break and then launched his three-hour charge to the jury.

Some of his instructions were right from the judge's instruction manual. In his monotone, Judge Ferguson defined homicide, *culpable homicide,* indecent assault, and *circumstantial evidence.*

"No one saw the prisoner kill Lynne Harper. The Crown, therefore, puts its case squarely on all of the circumstances and asks you to find from the circumstances that the accused is guilty."

To the testimony of children, he gave special note. In twos and threes, the children were brought in, reintroduced to the jury, and paraded out: Ronald Demaray, Dougie Oates, Paul Desjardine, Kenneth Geiger, Rod Harrington, Jocelyne Gaudet, Arnold George, Philip Burns, Richard Gellatly, Alan Oates, Gord Logan, Bryan Glover, Thomas Gillette. The aim, apparently, was to refresh the memories of the jury. The effect was likely the opposite — of adding to their weariness and confusion.

For almost three hours, Judge Ferguson reviewed the evidence. Who saw what. What doctors said about the time of death. About Steve's penis sores, his dirty underwear.

All of it was circumstantial, with three exceptions: the three young people — sworn witnesses — who told stories that supported Steve's version of events. If they were believed — even the judge was clear on this point — Steve was not guilty.

Neither the jury nor the judge knew that, hidden in the police files, there was a statement from a fourth witness who supported Steve's story. Karen Daum, then nine years old, the little girl who was hunting for turtles with Dougie Oates, had also been questioned by police. She even gave a signed statement in which she supported Dougie Oates's story, and had seen Steven and Lynne bicycle past the bridge. Years later, she recounted that police took her to the scene three times and badgered her to change her estimate of where she had seen them.

But Karen stuck to her story; and predictably, the Crown never called her for a witness. Since laws at the time did not require *full disclosure*, the Crown and the police did not reveal the existence of her statement to the defence. Donnelly did not call her as a witness because he did not know of her story.

Even as an unsworn witness, her appearance might have corroborated the stories of the others.

Finally, the judge came to the point the jury had been waiting for.

". . . You are now free to retire, gentlemen, and consider your verdict. The sheriff will look after your dinner."

• • •

Life is never quite that simple, of course.

The jury had barely returned to the jury room when the judge called them back for clarification. Defence attorney Frank Donnelly had objected to a number of points made by the judge. Before two hours had passed, the jury had been called back a total of three times and returned once on their own for clarification.

At 10:05 p.m. the jury filed back into the courtroom and took their seats. Floorboards creaked. The courthouse crowd sat in silence.

The court registrar stood.

"Gentlemen of the jury, have you agreed upon your verdict?"

The foreman of the jury also rose.

"No, My Lord, we have not."

Judge Ferguson sat back in surprise. "You have not?"

"We want some more information. Can I read this?"

"Yes."

The foreman read from a paper in his hand. "A redirection of evidence, corroborated or otherwise, of Lynne Harper and Steven Truscott being seen together on the bridge on the night of June the ninth."

The request was a key point. If Steve and Lynne were together on the bridge, Steve could not be guilty.

Judge Ferguson outlined the facts: that Dougie Oates

said Steve and Lynne were on the bridge headed north at about 7:30 p.m. Alan Oates and Gord Logan said the same.

But then he expanded on his answer.

He stated that Alan Oates "would make a shaky recognition of Steve on his bicycle at eight hundred feet." And that Gord Logan stood on a rock six hundred and forty feet east and had seen them through "a guard rail . . . forty inches high."

He also reminded them that Philip Burns walked south from the bridge and had not seen either Lynne or Steve. Nor had Jocelyne Gaudet and Arnold George.

"The going back and forth across the bridge is of very little important — very little importance, because the question is: did he kill her? That is the point in this case," the judge concluded.

Finally, at 10:45 p.m., the jury retired one last time.

Ten minutes later, at 10:55 p.m. — on a day that began at 10 a.m. — the jury returned.

This time, they had a verdict.

16

CHAPTER SIXTEEN

THE VERDICT IS IN

SEPTEMBER 30, 1959

The judge waited until the jury resettled into their seats. The wooden floors and chairs creaked. Otherwise, the room was pale with silence.

"Do you find the prisoner at the bar guilty or not guilty?" asked a court official.

The jury foreman rose.

"We find the defendant guilty as charged, with a plea for mercy."

Judge Ferguson looked at Steven. He said, "The prisoner stand up."

Steve, still the obedient kid, stood.

"Steven Murray Truscott, I have no alternative but to pass the following sentence upon you.

"The jury have found you guilty after a fair trial.

"The sentence of this court upon you is that you

be taken from this place . . ."

Steve Truscott became the youngest Canadian in history to be sentenced to death by hanging. So much for mercy.

17

CHAPTER SEVENTEEN

THE HOPE OF APPEAL

OCTOBER 1, 1959 - FEBRUARY 24, 1960

The day after the darkest of his life, Steve Truscott found it hard to hold on to hope.

He remained in the 117-year-old Goderich jail awaiting his hanging. It was to happen on December 8, 1959 — six months less a day after Lynne Harper disappeared.

One day in the fall, Steve could hear nearby construction: hammering, sawing, workers cursing.

His confused teen mind worked overtime. They were building a gallows, he thought. In the prison yard. He visualized a gallows as pictured in his textbook on English history. In his book, *The Steven Truscott Story*, he tells of wincing at every hammer blow. He stood on his bunk to peer out the small window, but could see nothing.

"The hammering went on all morning," he wrote.

"It was too soon. They wouldn't build a scaffold and leave it there for weeks. Or would they?"

That afternoon, when his favourite guard came on duty, he asked what was going on.

"They're repairing a house across the street," he was told.

"Weak with relief, I sank down on the edge of my bed and buried my face in my hands," he wrote.

Days, weeks went by.

Right after the conviction, Steven's lawyer held out two possibilities that would overturn the conviction.

First, an *appeal* to the Ontario Court of Appeal. That may be successful, he said, for several reasons: the jury was wrong, the evidence didn't support a guilty finding, and/or the judge had misled the jury.

Second, the grounds for a mistrial were provided early in the trial during the discussion over Steve's statement to police. At the time, the judge had chastised the Crown attorney for mentioning the statement. He had said that if Steve's statement was not introduced — and it was not — then there were clear grounds for a mistrial.

But three days after the jury verdict, lawyer Frank Donnelly was named a judge.

Steve's family hired a new lawyer, John O'Driscoll, to

file the appeal before the Ontario Court of Appeal.

Meanwhile, the Steven Truscott story changed from a legal story to a political one. For although the law said the teen must hang, the political system allowed for exceptions.

In a famous poem, "Requiem for a Fourteen-year-old," *Toronto Star* columnist Pierre Berton gave the story a voice. A nationally known figure himself, Berton took issue not only with the sentence — death is not nice — but with the pretense involved.

"We'll only pretend he's going to die," the poem said. Berton's poem was clear: Canada would not execute Steve. Everyone but Steve Truscott knew that — and we wouldn't tell him until the last minute, Berton's poem predicted.

On November 20, with his execution only eighteen days away, Steve received one small piece of good news: his hanging had been postponed.

Not cancelled — merely postponed, pending his appeal.

Even the court system seemed to realize that the appeal wouldn't do Steve much good if he were dead. Christmas in a jail cell came and went.

On January 18, 1960, Steve Truscott turned fifteen years old.

Three days later, the Ontario Court of Appeal handed down a decision:

Appeal denied.

The several judges on the panel admitted that mistakes were made, but not enough to overturn the verdict.

The very next day, the Government of Canada commuted his sentence from hanging to life in prison.

Happy birthday, Steve.

O'Driscoll immediately said he would appeal to the Supreme Court of Canada. A month later, on February 22, 1960, he filed the appeal.

This time there was no long, dragged-out process. Two days later, the appeal was denied. Today, similar appeals are granted automatically.

The Steve Truscott that the OPP arrested on June 13, 1959 was quiet, polite, and helpful. He tried hard to help police in their investigation. He never showed frustration. Even under arrest and in jail, his attitude didn't seem to change.

One guard at Goderich, who had been with Steve for three months, told a friend that if Steve was guilty, he should receive an acting award.

But systems are systems.

Special arrangements had been made for Steve.

Because of his age, he would spend his sentence in the Ontario Training School for Boys in Guelph until he turned eighteen.

When it came time for Steve to leave the old pioneer jail in Goderich — his home for nine months — he was led out in shackles and chains. On the way to Kingston, for one overnight stay, he was paraded into a public restaurant still in chains. People stared.

Prisoners are prisoners.

Steve spent one night in the Kingston Penitentiary. The next day he was transported west again, over the same 340-kilometre route, from Kingston to Guelph.

At the Ontario Training School, life was more relaxed. He was able to visit with his family without bars between them for the first time since his arrest, Steve completed his first two years of high school. He spent two years in the machine shop, laying the foundation for his later career as a millwright.

At the school, Steve also showed his true personality. Guards came to know him, and to like him. One cook became so attached to this quiet boy that she offered her driveway to the Truscotts to park their trailer so they had a place to stay when they were visiting him.

As Steve began serving his life sentence, the legal system began to close the case files. In 1962, the Ontario

Provincial Police ordered all of the evidence files destroyed.

But while Steve tried to wrestle a normal life out his nightmare, his case had not been forgotten. Among those who became interested in the case was a writer from Toronto. Isabel LeBourdais thought the story of a young teen sentenced for murder would make a good magazine article.

She underestimated the size of her project — which, in the end, would challenge Canada's legal and political systems.

18

CHAPTER EIGHTEEN

A BOOK CREATES MORE HOPE

MARCH 1966

Isabel LeBourdais was a stay-at-home mom. In the early 1960s, that was not unusual.

What first drew her to the Truscott case was the sentence: hanging. She was against the death penalty.

She also had a child of her own, a few months old, and had to wonder what kind of a legal system could sentence a child to death.

She talked to lawyers. To police. To residents of the RCAF base at Clinton. To the Truscott family.

She obtained copies of the original trial transcript — more than 1,600 pages of testimony from witnesses and arguments from lawyers. To that, she added the transcript of the preliminary hearing.

She read.

Her doubts piled up.

How could a young man — quiet, polite, well-liked — commit such a crime? To take a classmate into the woods, in broad daylight, within earshot of dozens of people, and there commit the most brutal and ugly crime imaginable — and then to emerge, minutes later unruffled, not even breaking into a sweat? To continue as though nothing had happened?

It didn't make sense. Worse, the trial didn't make sense. The Crown had insisted that Truscott had given Lynne Harper a ride on his bike. That he had taken her along the county road. At the tractor trail, he had taken her into Lawson's woods.

The Crown story placed several other children less than sixty metres away — the length of a hockey rink. They had been looking for both Lynne and Steve. In such a setting, in a woods in which sound travelled clearly in the damp evening air, he had raped and murdered her. Or murdered and raped — the Crown was never clear on the order. Then he had broken off three branches, each wider than a man's thumb, and placed them over her body.

He did all this quietly, while people passed by on the county road.

He had supposedly assaulted her so violently that she bled freely from a wound in her back. He had then carefully removed her shoes, socks, shorts and panties and placed them neatly near her body, dropping the panties in the process. In this frantic time, this boy had apparently had time to zip up her shorts, and fold them neatly.

And he was supposed to have done this without getting even one drop of blood on his pants, shirt, or shoes.

Another fact: a government scientist had testified at the trial that Lynne's shorts had dirt (mud) on them from a variety of sites in the area — but none from Lawson's woods. She had left home with clean shorts.

The murderer had left only indistinct footprints on the ground.

Impossible, she thought.

She talked to eleven of the twelve jurors: how did they arrive at a guilty verdict?

What they said stunned her.

The jurors found Steve guilty because:

• he looked back at jurors and would not avert his eyes;
• he showed no signs of remorse;
• the pathologist, Dr. Penistan, testified without looking at notes (so he must have known his stuff);
• Steve did not cry about the horrid stuff he had done.

One juror said he had no doubt from the beginning. Another, though, had a disturbing thought. The neatness with which the clothes were set down, and the branches covering the body, "seemed sort of strange."

"Do you think he could be innocent?" he asked LeBourdais.

LeBourdais said that was possible.

The juror suggested if that was true, the jury had "made a mistake — a terrible mistake."

The neatness bothered LeBourdais, too. Steve was a typical teen. His own room at home was a disaster area.

LeBourdais talked to the editor of *Maclean's* — a Canadian national weekly magazine. They waffled on the idea of publishing an article on the subject. Anything critical of courts could been seen as contempt of court, they said.

McClelland & Stewart, the largest Canadian book publisher, expressed some interest. By now, her files on the case had grown beyond the scope of a magazine article. She wanted to publish a book about Truscott's case. Jack McClelland, the publisher, was a family friend.

But McClelland consulted lawyers, and lawyers consulted lawyers, and all urged caution. The legal system does not like outsiders messing with verdicts.

They, too, worried about contempt of court.

For contempt, writers, publishers, even lawyers could be jailed.

Isabel LeBourdais had a greater disadvantage: she was a woman. Simply put, women in the 1960s were as not as likely to be taken seriously. As defence lawyer Frank Donnelly had told Steven's mother, women were thought to be "too emotional" to deal logically with the facts of the case.

At the time, few lawyers were women, and even fewer were judges. Or politicians. Or police. Society seemed more comfortable with women who worked in "traditional jobs." Law and journalism were not on that list.

Meanwhile, LeBourdais continued her research. She talked to residents on the air base, to the child witnesses, to anyone with an interest in the case. Her sense of social injustice grew.

Dan Truscott had been transferred to Ottawa a month after the arrest, even before the preliminary hearing. That was not fair. The jurors had prejudged Steve's guilt. Not fair. In her study, she ran directly into another frustration: the RCAF appeared to be actively discouraging inquiries. Air force personnel seemed to be split, with officers and their families feeling the guilty verdict was the right verdict, and enlisted people supporting Steve's innocence.

Lynne Harper's father had been an officer, Steve's father an enlisted man.

Three witnesses supported Steve's story of what happened that night.

Crown witnesses appeared to change their stories.

The story had to be told.

"No," said her publishers. "We won't publish unless you stick only to the facts. Don't start a fight with the court system."

But much of LeBourdais's book took on the process and the verdict head-on. She would not water down her criticism.

"Then there will be no book," McClelland & Stewart said.

LeBourdais approached a British publisher with a reputation for taking on edgy causes. Her book, *The Trial of Steve Truscott,* was published in 1966 in England by Victor Gollancz Ltd.

Almost right away, McClelland & Stewart followed with a Canadian edition.

The storm in Canada was immediate. Steve Truscott again became a household name. Isabel LeBourdais became a media star — and the first person in Canada to say the word "penis" on national television. In a television interview, she was discussing the details of the lesions on

Truscott's penis — originally thought to be proof of his guilt, and eventually shown to be a skin condition that continued to bother him.

In the media storm, a CBC television personality lost his job for weeping during an interview with Steve's mother. Politicians were chastised for taking sides.

Reluctantly, the Government of Canada referred the whole matter to the Supreme Court with a single mandate: if the appeal in 1960 had been granted, what would the court have decided?

It was a limited scope, and one many viewed as absurd.

But it was better than nothing.

Steve Truscott got his hopes up again.

19

CHAPTER NINETEEN

STEVE TELLS HIS STORY

OCTOBER 5, 1966 - MAY 4, 1967

During the 1966 and 1967 Supreme Court hearing, Steve Truscott told his story in court for the first time.

For the hearing, he had been transferred briefly from Collins Bay Penitentiary in Kingston to Ottawa.

Unprepared and shy, Steve faltered on the stand. He was always a quiet person, and his voice was weak. Several times, judges had to tell him to speak up. The intimidating setting at the Supreme Court did not help.

Besides his weak voice, Steve had one other problem: his memory. It was now almost seven years from the original events. Steve had sat through two weeks of conflicting testimony in his original trial. Also, he had virtually no preparation for the hearing. Unlike his one-time buddy, Butch George, he had no "cheat sheet" or prepared statement. He had no opportunity to review his original statement nor to review the court transcripts from the original trial.

In his testimony at the Supreme Court, Steve said he remembered giving Lynne a ride to the highway the night she died. But he did not remember seeing Richard Gellatly or many others that evening. He remembered seeing the 1959 Chev. He remembered seeing Gord Logan and Dougie Oates — but he couldn't remember their testimony at his trial.

In 1965, Steve had applied for parole. Now, even that came back to bite him.

In the application, Steve had written: "... please grant me one chance to make a success of my life and prove that one dreadful mistake ..."

To the prosecutor, this could mean only one thing: Steve was admitting his guilt. But Steve was only trying to provide the parole board with what they wanted to hear. Prison "wisdom" said parole was unlikely without admission of guilt. But to Steve, the "dreadful mistake" was the jury's verdict.

The court heard from experts who stated that the time of death could have been as late as midnight on June 9; that the penis lesions were due to a skin condition Truscott suffered from for years; that the body was likely moved after death and placed in the woods.

The defence trotted out experts to say the time of death could not be set from stomach contents. The Crown trotted out experts to say it could. This was not unlike the original trial.

One expert for the Crown was missing: Dr. Penistan, the pathologist who did the autopsy, did not testify. Steve's defence team did not know it, but in the year before the hearing, Dr. Penistan had changed his ideas on the time of death. He had concluded that Lynne Harper likely died after 8 p.m., maybe as late as midnight.

This meant that Steve Truscott could not be the killer.

But the Supreme Court hearing would never hear Dr. Penistan say this.

Steve's appearance before the Supreme Court backfired. In their final judgment, the court said that "part of his testimony . . . simply cannot be believed."

The court denied the appeal by an 8-1 decision.

Truscott was crushed. His last hope had disappeared.

• • •

One small glimmer of hope did emerge from the Supreme Court.

Unlike trials, a Supreme Court requires a panel of judges to review the legal processes involved. The Supreme Court was a panel of eight judges headed by The Honourable Robert Taschereau, Chief Justice of Canada.

Justice Emmett Hall wrote a dissenting opinion. He did not agree with the others. Justice Hall, incidentally, became known in Canada as one of the authors of our health-care system.

"The trial was not conducted according to law," Justice Hall wrote. "There were grave errors in the trial. Nothing that transpired on the hearing in this court or any evidence tendered before this court can be used to give validity to what was an invalid trial."

His judgment had nothing to do with guilt or innocence. He simply said the trial was not fair, and was not conducted according to law.

"The only remedy for a bad trial is a new trial," he wrote.

But Justice Hall was only one of eight Supreme Court judges on the case. His opinion was a legal footnote. In such cases, the majority rules.

Steve had run out of options.

He was twenty-one years old and faced life in prison.

20

CHAPTER TWENTY

AN ALMOST NORMAL LIFE

OCTOBER 21, 1969 - MARCH 29, 2000

In 1963, five days before his eighteenth birthday, Steven had been transferred from the relaxed atmosphere of the Ontario Training School to "hard" time: Collins Bay Penitentiary in Kingston, Ontario. He had been given a suit "three sizes too big" and a small bit of freedom that he cherished: he made the trip from Guelph to Kingston without handcuffs.

It was a stark contrast to the shackles and chains he had endured three years earlier.

It was from Kingston that he made the trip to Ottawa for his Supreme Court hearing. After the court decision was announced, Steve swallowed his bitter disappointment and got on with his life — as much as one can, under maximum security. He made friends; played baseball (third base); learned to be a millwright; became a broadcaster in the prison radio station.

In 1967, he was transferred to the nearby Farm Annex in Kingston. This gave him considerably more freedom, along with the physical challenge of farm work. Since his days on the Lawson farm, he considered himself a country boy.

After ten years in reform school and penitentiary, he had an unblemished record. He had earned the trust of the guards and prison staff.

Life went on. His parents, stressed by ten years of legal battles, divorced.

In 1969, Steve was granted parole. He moved in with parole officer Mac Stienburg, near Kingston. While there, Isabel LeBourdais introduced him to a girl in Guelph who had taken a strong interest in the case and had campaigned for his freedom. Her name was Marlene. Eventually, they would marry.

But parole comes with strings attached.

The terms of his parole required him to live under an assumed, or fake, name. Only a few of his closest friends knew his real identity.

He couldn't leave the country. He couldn't move without permission.

And he always carried the reputation of being a convicted killer.

In 1971, working with journalist Bill Trent, Steve published his story up to his parole in 1969 in the book *The Steven Truscott Story.*

In 1974, after five years on parole, Steve had some parole conditions lifted. He no longer had to report regularly to his parole officer.

But the conviction — and the injustice it symbolized — still rankled.

He and Marlene began raising a family. Lesley was born in 1971; Ryan two years later; and Devon in 1979.

Raising children with a deep, dark family secret had its challenges. How much do you tell the children, and when?

Their daughter, Lesley, was in high school when she found out.

Unknown to her parents, Lesley was at the school library one day when she discovered a 1979 book, *Who Killed Lynne Harper?*, a reissue of *The Steven Truscott Story.* Lesley flipped through the pages and was surprised to find Truscott family photos in the book. She found many of her aunts and uncles.

Two years later, when her mother had decided that it was time she learned the truth, Lesley looked at the pile of books on the coffee table and said, "Mom, I know."

Another time, when she was in grade eleven, Lesley's class was studying law.

One of the topics was the Truscott case.

The teacher impressed on the class the unfairness he felt had been imposed on the process.

After class, Lesley approached her teacher. She said she hoped the class would not discuss the Truscott case again. She said it made her uncomfortable. Her teacher said the case made him uncomfortable as well, knowing that an innocent boy could spend ten years in jail.

Lesley said she had an additional reason: Steve Truscott was her father.

The stunned teacher got to meet Steve Truscott the next day.

Once the children had grown, the need to shelter them lessened. Instead, for both Steve and Marlene, something else grew: the need to clear the Truscott name.

Finally, in the 1990s, a number of forces converged. A radio reporter whom Marlene had met years before, when the Bill Trent book was released, now worked for the CBC. She had kept in contact with her.

One day, the reporter asked if Steve would be interested in doing a national TV show on his case.

By then, a new organization had begun to make a name for itself in Canadian news: the Association in

Defence of the Wrongly Convicted (AIDWYC).

Under the direction of lawyer James Lockyer, AIDWYC had started to get results in Canadian courts. Using legal procedures, supported by up-to-date science including DNA evidence, convictions were being overturned.

Guy Paul Morin.

David Milgaard.

Donald Marshall, Jr.

Clayton Johnston.

And in the U.S., Hurricane Carter.

Miscarriages of justice, it seemed, were not that rare.

DNA evidence had cleared Morin; if that science had existed in 1959, there would have been no conviction. Could that same science now free Steven?

Could exposure in the media help push for his injustice to be righted?

Maybe.

Steve was reluctant. He knew what it was like to get his hopes up and have them dashed.

Marlene had been his main supporter. Now, Lockyer joined the argument. This would be, he told Steve, the last chance to clear his name.

Finally, after talking with their children, Steve and Marlene agreed: let's do it.

With AIDWYC, and *the fifth estate,* a CBC public affairs program known for thorough research, Steve signed an agreement that any results of the investigation would be public information.

If DNA confirmed his conviction, the public would be told.

If new evidence did the same, the public would know.

Steve said he had nothing to hide, nothing to lose, and his name and his freedom to gain.

On March 29, 2000, CBC's *the fifth estate* broadcast a documentary that refuelled the debate about his innocence.

21

CHAPTER TWENTY-ONE

THE FINAL COURT BATTLE

NOVEMBER 28, 2001 - AUGUST 28, 2007

The battle to clear Steven Truscott's name began with a one-two punch.

First was the documentary on *the fifth estate*. A year later came the publication of yet another book. This one, *Until You Are Dead*, by Julian Sher of *the fifth estate* staff, added to the argument that Steve was innocent and the miscarriage of justice had to be made right.

The book and the television show brought the case back into public prominence — this time captivating people who had not been born when Steve and Lynne took that fateful bicycle ride.

James Lockyer and AIDWYC worked on the case. In 2001, they appealed to the government to have the case reopened. A new trial would have freed Steve Truscott.

"The night before the decision came out," said

Marlene Truscott, "I told Steve that I firmly believed that this was to be the last night he would go to sleep as a convicted murderer."

More than a hundred well-wishers had gathered at the Truscott home the day the decision arrived. Steve received a phone call. The room went silent.

But when Steve turned to his family and guests, the look on his face told the story.

Instead of a new trial, Justice Minister Cotler had referred the case to retired judge Fred Kaufman for review. Marlene later wrote: "We must now face 'another bump in the road' as my husband stated . . . It will involve more time and more expense but hopefully will be worth it in the end."

Steve Truscott had now been battling for justice for forty-four years.

It took two years before Kaufman's report was completed; another six months before an appeal by the Ontario Court of Appeal was ordered; and a further ten months before the Kaufman report was released to the public.

In his report, Justice Kaufman said that the new evidence presented by AIDWYC cast doubt on Truscott's conviction, but it was not sufficient to pronounce him innocent. However, "viewing the evidence cumulatively, there is clearly a reasonable basis for concluding that a miscarriage of justice, as earlier defined, likely occurred." This was Kaufman's way of saying Truscott was likely wrongfully convicted.

Justice works slowly.

In April 2006, Lynne Harper's body was exhumed. In other cases of wrongful conviction, DNA had been a clincher. DNA (deoxyribonucleic acid) is a genetic marker. It is found in blood, saliva, and semen. The hope was that even after all these years, they would find traces to show Steve could not be the rapist and murderer. But no DNA remained. The exhumation provided nothing to help Steve.

Over a period of another year and a half, the Ontario Court of Appeal summoned witnesses and reviewed all new evidence.

As before, experts argued the time of death. This time, though, the defence team unearthed three different copies of Dr. Penistan's original autopsy report.

Dr. Penistan himself, they found, had on his own initiative undertaken "an agonizing reappraisal" of the time of death as far back as 1966. This helped explain why he had not appeared as an expert in the Supreme Court review. The death, Dr. Penistan had concluded, could have been four or more hours later than the narrow 7:15-7:45 p.m. window he had given originally.

The key witness who saw Truscott on the bridge, Dougie Oates, repeated his story — that he had been within a few feet of Lynne and Steve as they crossed the bridge. He had been hunting turtles with Karen Daum (now Karen Jutzi).

From Ontario Archive files, defence lawyers found Karen's original statement to police. In 1959, she had told police that she, too, had seen the pair cross the bridge. Later, she said the police had tried to persuade her three times to change her story about where she had seen them.

Additional documents, including original statements to police and case notes by OPP investigators, all supported Truscott's innocence.

Finally, on August 28, 2007, the court delivered a decision.

This time, Steve was on Highway 401 when he took a call from his lawyers on his son's cell phone: "You are free. No more parole. You've been acquitted by the court."

"I will never forget the weight being lifted from my shoulders," Steve wrote later. "It is hard to explain the feeling of relief after forty-six years of bearing the wrongful conviction and then suddenly, in a moment's time, it is all over."

After forty-seven years, eleven months, and two days, he was free at last.

A few months later, the Ontario Government officially acknowledged the miscarriage of justice that had taken away a man's life for almost half a century. The government awarded him $6.5 million in compensation.

22

WHO KILLED LYNNE HARPER?

One question remains: who *did* kill Lynne Harper?

Even if a killer were found, fifty-two years later, the evidence necessary for a trial is no longer available. Witnesses have died. Physical evidence — what little there was — has been destroyed.

Any answers are now little more than guesses.

Over the years, a number of possibilities have been raised. *The fifth estate* puts air force sergeant Alexander Kalichuk high on the list. Others have named two brothers and a friend who were painting in the area that day; or an airman who was later accused of trying to rape his own daughter in the woods.

The neat pile of clothing near the body suggests another possibility. Could the killer have been a ranking official on the air base? Someone who took part in the search that found the body — and stayed near the murder scene until the body was removed?

The killer could have even encouraged another officer to have the body covered with jackets, ensuring a
contaminated scene in case he was later linked to the
killing. Perhaps it was the killer himself who kept nudg-
ing police to see only Steve Truscott as a suspect.

Unfortunately, we will never know.

A WORD OF THANKS . . .

The story of Steven Truscott is a story of children. It is obviously a story of the gross injustice done to Steven Truscott. But the happenings that June evening in 1959 did injustice to a whole village of children. The stories of child witnesses were twisted to support legal arguments. Uncertainties were used as wedges to create a change in the "facts."

In preparing this book, I used primary sources for all material. This includes original transcripts of the preliminary hearing, the trial, the various appeals, and Supreme Court hearings. My thanks in this to the CBC online archives, and online files from the Association in Defence of the Wrongly Convicted.

Special thanks to farmer Bob Lawson, who generously provided time on a June afternoon to clarify key points.

One cannot spend a year or more with this story without developing a deep appreciation for those who have spent months, years, and decades with it — and to those who continue to live with it to this day.

Although this story points out failures in our justice system, it must also come with a special salute to lawyers such as James Lockyer, Marlys Edwardh, and the team at the Association in Defence of the Wrongly Convicted who demonstrated the role of lawyers at their shining best.

Isabel LeBourdais, Bill Trent, and Julian Sher with the team at *the fifth estate* prove that journalism, properly and carefully executed, has the ability to right wrongs and be a force for good in the world. May their examples inspire the career choices of young people.

WITH THANKS TO:

The Association in Defence of the Wrongly Convicted (AIDWYC);

The CBC program *the fifth estate*;

The Ontario Council of the Arts for their support;

And to Jim Lorimer and Pam Hickman for helping me to colour inside the lines.

GLOSSARY

ACQUITTAL: the verdict when someone accused of a crime is found not guilty.

ADVERSARIAL SYSTEM: a legal system where one person (usually a lawyer) argues each side's position before a jury or judge, who decide the case.

APPEAL: a request to review a case that has already been decided in court.

CIRCUMSTANTIAL EVIDENCE: evidence that does not directly connect someone to a crime, but places him or her at the scene or suggests they may have been involved. It cannot be accepted as proof unless all other explanations can be ruled out.

CONVICTION: the verdict when someone accused of a crime is found guilty.

CULPABLE HOMICIDE: an offence which involves the illegal killing of a person either with or without intention. In Canada, both murder and manslaughter are culpable homicides, but a death resulting from self-defence is not.

CROWN ATTORNEY: the lawyer acting for the government, or "the Crown," in court proceedings. They are the prosecutors in Canada's legal system.

DEFENDANT: the person who has been formally accused of and charged with committing a crime.

FIRST-DEGREE MURDER: the planned or deliberate killing of another human being. In Canada, there are thirteen conditions under which someone can be charged with first-degree murder. Murder while committing or attempting to commit aggravated sexual assault is one of them.

FULL DISCLOSURE: revealing important or requested evidence to the other side in a trial. In 1991, the Supreme Court of Canada ruled that the Crown had a duty to reveal its evidence to the defence before trial. Before 1991, disclosure was voluntary.

JURY SYSTEM: A criminal trial is decided by a group of twelve randomly selected citizens from the province in which the trial is held. All twelve must agree on a verdict.

PRELIMINARY HEARING: a hearing held to decide if there is enough evidence for a trial. This is held after the accused has been charged with a crime.

PROSECUTOR: the lawyer acting for the prosecution, usually the state (in Canada, the Crown). The prosecutor tries to prove the defendant is guilty.

SEQUESTERED: isolated from others. A judge may order that the jury be kept away from news, media, and other sources that might sway their decision. They must remain sequestered until the trial is over.

TESTIMONY: the statement of a witness under oath.

VERDICT: the decision of the jury at the end of a trial, usually guilty or not guilty.

FURTHER READING

For the reader who wishes to find out more about this fascinating case, a rich resource of documents, news articles, and videos is available online through the following links:

www.cbc.ca/news/background/truscott/documents.
  html

www.cbc.ca/fifth/truscott/

INTERMEDIATE LEVEL

LeBourdais, Isabel. *The Trial of Steven Truscott*. Toronto: McClelland & Stewart, 1966.

Trent, Bill, with Steven Truscott. *Who Killed Lynne Harper?* Montreal: Optimum Publishing Company Ltd., 1979.

Sher, Julian. *Until You Are Dead*. Toronto: Vintage Canada, 2002.

PHOTO CREDITS

We gratefully acknowledge the following sources for permission to reproduce the images contained within this book:

The London Free Press: p. 79, 80 (bottom), 81, 82, 83 (top), 84

Sher, Julian. *Until You Are Dead*. Toronto: Vintage Canada, 2002. p. 80 (top), 83 (bottom)

INDEX